C000319590

Vegetarian

it's not all beans and tofu

MURDOCH BOOKS

Vegetarian cuisine has been maligned for far too long, considered the province of hairy hippies and health-food freaks. While there are many worthy reasons for choosing meat-free meals, you don't need to be a dedicated vegetarian to enjoy the fabulous dishes in this book, all of which have been chosen solely and unashamedly for their sheer great taste and vibrant flavours — nothing dull, bland or unsatisfying here! Drawing fresh inspiration from around the globe, our handpicked recipes will tantalise your tastebuds and take them on a gastronomic journey through the world's great cuisines. From enticing snacks and starters to hearty repasts, within these pages a feast of flavours awaits.

Contents

06 *Snacks, soups and starters*

Feeling peckish? Our light menu offerings in this chapter bring you the world on a plate. Tuck into a bowl of Chinese hot and sour soup, or even a chilled Moroccan carrot and capsicum soup ... or why not nibble on some sushi, Vietnamese rice paper rolls or Syrian lentil pizzas? The possibilities are delightfully surprising.

96 *Mains*

Our culinary adventure continues with tastebud teasers and palate pleasers such as Tunisian vegetable stew, polenta and provolone soufflé with red wine–rosemary capsicum, pumpkin gnocchi with three-cheese sauce, turlu turlu with roasted haloumi, mushroom and spinach lasagne, Mexican bean casserole on cornbread, five-spice braised eggplant with tofu and bok choy ... and so many more!

Snacks, soups and starters

Steamed Chinese pearl balls • Pumpkin and polenta chips • Carrot pierogi with dill sour cream • Syrian lentil pizzas • Fried eggplant, mozzarella and basil sandwiches • Olive, goat's cheese and potato triangles • Blue cheese and hazelnut butter pumpernickel stacks • Black pepper, fennel and Marsala biscotti • Capsicum sformato with radicchio and olive salad • Haloumi croûtes with onion, raisin and oregano marmalade • Chilled Moroccan carrot and capsicum soup • Chargrilled vegetable platter with roasted garlic aïoli • Vegetarian galloping horses • Cheddar soda bread with pickled cauliflower • Asparagus and snow pea tempura • Mushroom caviar with olive bread • Vegetarian sushi • Chilled tomato mousse with sesame pastries • Split pea samosas • Mini pumpkin pancakes with slow-roasted tomatoes and creamy pesto • Roast parsnip, pumpkin, chestnut and pear salad • Roast tomato, sweet potato and orange soup with basil oil • Braised beetroot salad with goat's cheese croutons • Broad bean and haloumi fritters with walnut tarator • Miso broth with tofu and mushrooms • Quinoa and vegetable soup • Middle Eastern burghul salad • Soba noodle salad with tofu, radish and sesame • Banh xeo • Tomato salad with mint pepper dressing, raita and poppadoms • Lemongrass, corn and coconut soup • Thai tofu salad • Red lentil koftas with tahini garlic sauce • Thai eggs with sweet and spicy sauce • Vietnamese rice paper rolls • Barley, celery and yoghurt soup • Radicchio salad with fennel, grapefruit, blue cheese and almonds • Indonesian spring rolls • Chinese hot and sour soup • Mushroom salad with ciabatta croutons and mint salsa verde • Warm jerusalem artichoke and potato purée with hazelnut dukkah • Stuffed vine leaves with egg and lemon sauce • Stuffed tomatoes with baked yoghurt • Fritto misto with tarragon mayonnaise

Preparation time: 30 minutes
plus at least 6 hours soaking

Cooking time: 45 minutes

Serves: 4

Steamed Chinese pearl balls

300 g (10½ oz/1½ cups) white sticky
   (glutinous) rice
8 dried shiitake mushrooms
1 spring onion (scallion), finely chopped
40 g (1½ oz/¼ cup) finely chopped
   tinned water chestnuts
1 small carrot, finely grated (about
   80 g/2¾ oz/½ cup)
60 g (2¼ oz) firm tofu, drained and cut
   into 1 cm (½ inch) cubes
2 teaspoons grated fresh ginger
1 tablespoon finely chopped coriander
   (cilantro) leaves
2 teaspoons soy sauce
¼ teaspoon sesame oil
½ teaspoon sea salt
1 egg white
2 tablespoons cornflour (cornstarch)

Sesame ginger dipping sauce
2 tablespoons Chinese black vinegar
½ teaspoon sesame oil
1 tablespoon finely shredded fresh ginger
1 teaspoon sugar

Place the rice in a bowl and cover with cold water. Leave to soak for at least 6 hours, or preferably overnight.

Put the mushrooms in a heatproof bowl and cover with boiling water. Leave to soak for 30 minutes, then drain well. Trim the stalks from the mushrooms, then finely chop the caps and set aside.

Drain the rice well. Remove about ½ cup of the rice, spread it on a tray and set aside.

In a double-boiler, bring 750 ml (26 fl oz/ 3 cups) water to the boil over high heat. Place a perforated insert or steaming basket in the top of the double-boiler and line it with a clean kitchen cloth. Spread the remaining rice over the cloth. Cover tightly and cook for 15–20 minutes, or until the rice is tender.

Spray a heatproof plate with cooking oil spray. Place the cooked rice in a bowl. Add the remaining ingredients (excluding the reserved rice) to the cooked rice and mix well, adding a little more cornflour if necessary to bind the mixture together. Shape tablespoons of the mixture into balls, then roll the balls lightly over the reserved uncooked rice. Place one batch of balls 1 cm (½ inch) apart on the prepared plate.

Preheat the oven to 120°C (235°F/Gas ½). Line a baking tray with baking paper.

Place the plate in a steamer or bamboo basket set over a saucepan of boiling water. Cover and steam for 10–15 minutes, or until cooked through. Transfer to the baking tray, cover with foil and place in the oven to keep warm. Repeat with the remaining rice balls.

Meanwhile, put all the sesame ginger dipping sauce ingredients in a small bowl. Mix until the sugar has dissolved and the sauce is well combined.

Serve the balls with the sesame ginger dipping sauce.

Sticky rice has a high starch content, a little like arborio. It can be long or short-grained and comes in black, white and even red varieties. Although it is gluten-free, it is called glutinous rice as the grains become gluey and stick together during cooking. It is the type of rice used in sticky rice puddings.

Pumpkin and polenta chips

olive or vegetable oil, for brushing and
  deep-frying
750 ml (26 fl oz/3 cups) vegetable stock
1 teaspoon sea salt
250 g (9 oz/2 cups) coarsely grated
  pumpkin (winter squash)
250 g (9 oz/1⅔ cups) polenta
30 g (1 oz) unsalted butter, chopped
35 g (1¼ oz/⅓ cup) finely grated
  parmesan cheese
1 tablespoon finely chopped flat-leaf
  (Italian) parsley
1 teaspoon finely chopped rosemary

Herb mayonnaise

2 egg yolks
1 teaspoon dijon mustard
200 ml (7 fl oz) light olive oil
1 tablespoon lemon juice
1 handful flat-leaf (Italian) parsley, finely
  chopped
1 small handful basil leaves, chopped

To make the herb mayonnaise, place the egg yolks and mustard in a small food processor and blend until well combined. With the motor running, very slowly drizzle in one-third of the olive oil until well combined, then add the remaining oil in a thin steady stream until all the oil has been added and the mayonnaise is a thick consistency. Add the lemon juice and herbs and blend until well combined. Season to taste with sea salt, then cover and set aside until required.

Brush a 30 x 20 cm (12 x 8 inch) baking dish generously with oil.

Bring the stock to the boil in a large saucepan over high heat. Stir in the salt and grated pumpkin and reduce the heat to medium–low. Gradually add the polenta in a thin steady stream, whisking constantly until smooth. Cook, stirring constantly, for 15 minutes, or until the polenta is very thick and pulls away from the side of the pan. Remove from the heat and stir in the butter, parmesan and herbs. Season to taste.

Pour the polenta mixture into the baking dish, spreading it evenly. Leave to cool, then refrigerate for 1–2 hours, or until completely chilled and firm.

Turn the polenta out onto a cutting board. Trim the edges and cut into 20 evenly sized 'chips', each measuring about 8 x 1.5 cm x 1.5 cm (3¼ x ⅝ inch x ⅝ inch).

Preheat the oven to 120°C (235°F/Gas ½). In a frying pan, heat 1 cm (½ inch) oil over high heat until a small piece of polenta sizzles when dropped into the hot oil. Working in three or four batches, fry the polenta chips for 2 minutes on each side, or until golden brown, carefully turning them with a spatula. Remove and drain on paper towels and keep warm in the oven while frying the remaining batches.

Serve warm, with the herb mayonnaise.

Preparation time: 45 minutes
plus 20 minutes chilling

Cooking time: 50 minutes

Makes: 24

Carrot pierogi with dill sour cream

60 ml (2 fl oz/¼ cup) olive oil
1 brown onion, finely chopped
2 garlic cloves, crushed
4 carrots (about 400 g/14 oz),
    coarsely grated
2 hard-boiled eggs, peeled and
    finely chopped
125 g (4½ oz/½ cup) cottage cheese
2 tablespoons finely chopped flat-leaf
    (Italian) parsley, plus extra leaves,
    to garnish
1 tablespoon finely chopped dill, plus
    extra sprigs, to garnish
1 tablespoon snipped chives, plus extra
    lengths, to garnish
30 g (1 oz) butter

Pierogi dough
350 g (12 oz/2⅓ cups) plain (all-purpose)
    flour, plus extra, for dusting
2 eggs, lightly whisked
100 g (3½ oz) sour cream

Dill sour cream
100 g (3½ oz) sour cream
2 tablespoons finely chopped dill
1 tablespoon snipped chives
2 teaspoons lemon juice

To make the pierogi dough, place the flour in a large bowl. Mix together the eggs, sour cream and 60 ml (2 fl oz/¼ cup) water. Add to the flour and mix with a wooden spoon, gradually adding another 90 ml (3 fl oz) water until a slightly soft dough forms. Turn out onto a lightly floured surface and knead gently for 3–4 minutes until smooth, adding a little extra flour if the dough is sticky. Dust lightly with flour, cover with plastic wrap and refrigerate for 20 minutes.

Meanwhile, heat 1 tablespoon of the olive oil in a frying pan over medium–low heat. Add the onion and cook, stirring, for 8 minutes, or until softened. Add the garlic and carrot and cook for another 5 minutes, or until the carrot is tender. Transfer the mixture to a bowl, then gently stir in the egg, cottage cheese and herbs. Season to taste with sea salt and freshly ground black pepper and set aside.

Divide the dough in half. Roll one portion on a floured surface until 2 mm (1/16 inch) thick, using a little extra flour if the dough is sticky. Cut the dough into rounds using a 9 cm (3½ inch) cutter. Place 1 tablespoon of the carrot mixture on one half of each round. Brush the edges with water, fold the dough over to enclose the filling, then pinch the edges firmly to seal. Repeat with the remaining dough and carrot mixture.

Bring a large saucepan of water to the boil. Cook the pierogi, about 12 at a time, for 3–4 minutes, or until tender. Drain well.

Heat the remaining olive oil in a heavy-based non-stick frying pan over medium–high heat. Add the butter and heat until foaming. Cook the pierogi in batches for 1 minute on each side, or until golden.

To make the dill sour cream, combine the sour cream, dill and chives in a small serving bowl. Stir in the lemon juice and season to taste.

Serve the pierogi scattered with extra parsley dill and chives, with the dill sour cream.

Originally Polish peasant food, pierogi are unleavened half-moon dumplings that may be boiled, baked or fried. They usually contain a savoury filling, but can also enclose a sweet fruit filling to be enjoyed as a dessert. They are not suitable for freezing.

Syrian lentil pizzas

You can serve these little pizzas topped with a dollop of good Greek-style yoghurt and sprinkled with chopped parsley or coriander.

90 g (3¼ oz/½ cup) brown lentils
60 ml (2 fl oz/¼ cup) olive oil, plus extra, for drizzling
4 brown onions, chopped
50 g (1¾ oz/⅓ cup) pine nuts
½ teaspoon ground cinnamon
1 teaspoon ground allspice
3 ripe tomatoes, seeded and finely chopped
125 g (4½ oz/1 cup) crumbled feta cheese
1 tablespoon pomegranate molasses
2 lemons, cut into wedges

Pizza dough
225 g (8 oz/1½ cups) plain (all-purpose) flour
225 g (8 oz/1½ cups) wholemeal (whole-wheat) flour
2 teaspoons dried yeast
2 teaspoons salt
½ teaspoon sugar
2 tablespoons olive oil

To make the pizza dough, combine both flours, yeast, salt and sugar in a large bowl. Make a well in the centre. Combine the oil with 310 ml (10¾ fl oz/1¼ cups) lukewarm water. Add to the flour mixture and mix until a soft dough forms, adding another tablespoon of lukewarm water if necessary. Turn out onto a lightly floured surface and knead for 8–10 minutes, or until smooth and elastic. Place in an oiled bowl, turning to coat in the oil. Cover with plastic wrap and stand in a warm, draught-free place for 1 hour, or until doubled in size.

Meanwhile, place the lentils in a saucepan with 750 ml (26 fl oz/3 cups) cold water and bring to the boil over high heat. Reduce the heat to low, cover and simmer for 30 minutes, or until the lentils are very tender. Drain well.

Heat the olive oil in a non-stick frying pan over medium heat. Add the onion and cook, stirring, for 10 minutes, or until softened and light golden. Stir in the pine nuts, cinnamon and allspice and cook for 1 minute. Remove from the heat, then stir in the lentils, tomato, feta and pomegranate molasses. Season to taste with sea salt and freshly ground black pepper.

Preheat the oven to 200°C (400°F/Gas 6). Line two baking trays with baking paper. Knock down the pizza dough, then break off pieces the size of a golf ball (about 45 g/1½ oz each). Roll each one out on a lightly floured surface until 3 mm (⅛ inch) thick and about 12 cm (4½ inches) in diameter. Place the rounds on the baking trays and bake for 5 minutes. Remove from the oven and pierce several times with a fork to deflate.

Spread about 70 g (2½ oz/⅓ cup) of the lentil mixture over each round, leaving a 2 cm (¾ inch) border. Drizzle with a little extra olive oil and bake for 10–12 minutes, or until the bases are golden brown around the edges and cooked through.

Serve immediately, with the lemon wedges.

Preparation time: 30 minutes
plus 1 hour proving

Cooking time: 1 hour

Serves: 6
(makes 18)

Preparation time: 30 minutes
plus 20 minutes standing

Cooking time: 30 minutes

Serves: 4

Fried eggplant, mozzarella and basil sandwiches

2 eggplants (aubergines), about 700 g
    (1 lb 9 oz)
sea salt, for sprinkling
100 g (3½ oz) goat's cheese
100 g (3½ oz/⅔ cup) coarsely grated
    fresh mozzarella cheese
1 tablespoon snipped chives
1 handful basil leaves
75 g (2½ oz/½ cup) plain
    (all-purpose) flour
2 eggs
100 g (3½ oz/1 cup) dry breadcrumbs
2 tablespoons finely chopped flat-leaf
    (Italian) parsley
vegetable oil, for pan-frying
lemon wedges, to serve

Cut the eggplants into 5 mm (¼ inch) rounds. Spread them on a wire rack and sprinkle with sea salt. Set aside for 20 minutes, or until the eggplant slices are covered in water droplets. Rinse, then pat dry with paper towels.

Preheat the oven to 120°C (235°F/Gas ½).

In a small bowl, mix together the goat's cheese, mozzarella, chives and some freshly ground black pepper. Spread the mixture over half the eggplant slices, then top with basil leaves and another eggplant slice of the same size. Press gently to seal.

Spread the flour on a plate. Whisk the eggs in a wide shallow bowl. Toss the breadcrumbs and parsley together in a bowl and season to taste with sea salt and freshly ground black pepper.

Dip each eggplant 'sandwich' in the flour, shaking off any excess. Dip into the egg to coat well, then coat evenly with the breadcrumbs.

In a large non-stick frying pan, heat 1 cm (½ inch) oil over medium–high heat to 180°C (350°F) or until a cube of bread dropped into the oil browns in 15 seconds.

Working in batches, fry the eggplant sandwiches for 2 minutes on each side, or until golden brown, carefully turning them over with a spatula. Drain on paper towels and keep warm in the oven while cooking the remaining batches.

Serve immediately, with lemon wedges and some sea salt for sprinkling.

Buffalo mozzarella is made from the rich, nutritious milk of water buffalo. It has a better flavour than mozzarella made from cow's milk, so do use it in this dish if you can find it.
Instead of coating the 'sandwiches' with the breadcrumbs, you could use fine polenta.

Olive, goat's cheese and potato triangles

600 g (1 lb 5 oz) desiree or other
   all-purpose potatoes, peeled
   and chopped
2 tablespoons olive oil
1 large brown onion, finely chopped
2 garlic cloves, crushed
1½ teaspoons ground cumin
35 g (1¼ oz/¼ cup) pitted green
   olives, chopped
200 g (7 oz) soft goat's
   cheese, crumbled
2 tablespoons chopped mint
2 tablespoons chopped coriander
   (cilantro)
2 tablespoons chopped flat-leaf
   (Italian) parsley
12 sheets filo pastry
60 g (2¼ oz) butter, melted

Tomato and mint salad
250 g (9 oz) cherry tomatoes, halved
2 spring onions (scallions), finely chopped
2 tablespoons mint leaves

Preheat the oven to 180°C (350°F/Gas 4). Line two baking trays with baking paper.

Place the potatoes in a saucepan, cover with cold water and bring to the boil. Cook for 7–10 minutes, or until tender. Drain well, then transfer to a large bowl.

Heat the olive oil in a frying pan over medium heat. Add the onion and cook, stirring, for 5–8 minutes, or until softened. Add the garlic and cumin and cook, stirring, for 1 minute, or until aromatic.

Add the mixture to the potato, then mash with a fork to roughly break up the potato. Stir in the olives, cheese and herbs until well combined. Season to taste with sea salt and freshly ground black pepper.

Place one sheet of filo pastry on a cutting board. Brush with the melted butter and top with another sheet of pastry. Repeat to make a stack of three pastry sheets. Cut the pastry stack into four 10 cm (4 inch)-wide strips. Place 2 heaped tablespoons of the potato mixture at one end of each pastry strip. Fold the bottom right corner of the pastry up to form a triangle. Fold the parcel up again along the horizontal to enclose the filling. Continue folding along the pastry strip, keeping the triangle shape. Place the triangles on the baking trays and brush the tops with a little more melted butter. Repeat with the remaining pastry, butter and potato mixture to make 16 triangles.

Bake the triangles for 15–20 minutes, or until the pastry is lightly browned and crisp.

Meanwhile, combine the tomato and mint salad ingredients in a small bowl.

Serve the triangles hot, with the tomato and mint salad.

Preparation time: 30 minutes   Cooking time: 40 minutes   Serves: 4
(makes 16)

Preparation time: 15 minutes
plus 1 hour chilling

Cooking time: Nil

Makes: 12

Blue cheese and hazelnut butter pumpernickel stacks

45 g (1½ oz) butter, softened
100 g (3½ oz) soft mild blue cheese
2 tablespoons milk
2 tablespoons chopped roasted
   hazelnuts
1 tablespoon finely snipped chives
6 slices (280 g/10 oz) pumpernickel
   bread
quince paste, to serve

To make the filling, combine the butter, blue cheese and milk in a bowl. Beat with electric beaters until smooth and creamy, then stir in the hazelnuts and chives.

Lay two pumpernickel slices on a board. Spread one quarter of the filling evenly over each slice and top firmly with another slice of pumpernickel. Spread two more pumpernickel slices with the remaining filling, then top with the remaining pumpernickel.

Press the pumpernickel stacks down firmly; the layers should all be of the same thickness. Scrape any excess filling off the sides using a flat-bladed knife or spatula. Wrap in plastic wrap and refrigerate for 1 hour, or until the filling is firm.

Using a sharp knife dipped in hot water, cut the pumpernickel stacks into six even portions. Spoon about ½ teaspoon quince paste on top of each portion. Arrange on a serving plate and serve with drinks.

These pumpernickel stacks can be made up to a day ahead of serving but are not suitable for freezing.

Black pepper, fennel and Marsala biscotti

Marsala is a fortified wine from Marsala in Sicily that is produced in various degrees of sweetness. Dry Marsalas are used in savoury dishes and are enjoyed as an aperitif. Sweet Marsalas find their way into dessert dishes such as zabaglione and are also served with desserts. In this recipe, the Marsala gives the biscotti a slight earthy sweetness that teams well with the saltiness of the parmesan and olives.

375 g (13 oz/2½ cups) plain (all-purpose) flour
60 g (2¼ oz/⅓ cup) caster (superfine) sugar
1½ teaspoons baking powder
2 teaspoons cracked black pepper
1½ teaspoons sea salt
1½ teaspoons fennel seeds
125 ml (4 fl oz/½ cup) extra virgin olive oil
150 ml (5 fl oz) sweet Marsala
1 egg yolk
2 tablespoons sesame seeds
small parmesan cheese chunks, to serve
dried black olives, to serve

Preheat the oven to 180°C (350°F/Gas 4). Lightly grease a large baking tray.

In a large bowl, mix together the flour, sugar, baking powder, pepper, salt and fennel seeds.

Combine the olive oil and Marsala in a small bowl, then add to the flour mixture and mix with a wooden spoon until a firm dough forms.

Divide the dough in half, then cut each half into 12 even portions. Working on a floured surface and with one piece of dough at a time, use your hands to roll each piece into a rope about 12 cm (4½ inches) long. Form each rope into a ring shape, pressing the ends firmly to join. Place on the baking tray.

In a small bowl, beat the egg yolk with 1 tablespoon water, then brush over the biscotti. Sprinkle with the sesame seeds.

Bake for 20–25 minutes, or until the biscotti are light golden and cooked through. Remove to a wire rack to cool.

Serve with small chunks of parmesan and dried black olives.

✳ **Preparation time:** 35 minutes ✳ **Cooking time:** 25 minutes ✳ **Makes:** 24

Preparation time: 15 minutes   **Cooking time:** 1 hour 30 minutes   **Serves:** 4

Capsicum sformato with radicchio and olive salad

1½ tablespoons olive oil, plus extra, for brushing
1 red capsicum (pepper), thinly sliced
75 g (2½ oz) butter
75 g (2½ oz/½ cup) plain (all-purpose) flour
750 ml (26 fl oz/3 cups) milk
75 g (2½ oz/¾ cup) grated pecorino cheese
2 eggs, plus 2 egg yolks
½ teaspoon freshly grated nutmeg, or to taste

Radicchio and olive salad
60 ml (2 fl oz/¼ cup) olive oil
2 heads of radicchio, trimmed, washed and patted dry, then cut into 8 wedges each
60 g (2¼ oz/½ cup) pitted black olives, sliced
1 small handful small basil leaves
1 tablespoon red wine vinegar

Heat the olive oil in a frying pan over medium heat. Add the capsicum and cook, stirring, for 5–8 minutes, or until softened. Remove from the pan and set aside.

Melt the butter in a saucepan over medium heat. Stir in the flour until smooth, then cook, stirring occasionally, for 2 minutes. Remove from the heat, then gradually add the milk, whisking constantly until combined. Return the pan to medium heat and stir until the mixture thickens and boils. Reduce the heat to low and simmer for 10 minutes, stirring to prevent lumps from forming. Remove from the heat, cover the surface of the sauce with a round of baking paper and set aside to cool for 5 minutes.

Meanwhile, preheat the oven to 160°C (315°F/Gas 2–3). Brush four 185 ml (6 fl oz/¾ cup) ramekins with olive oil.

In a large bowl, combine the cooled béchamel sauce with the pecorino, eggs, egg yolks and nutmeg, then season to taste with sea salt and freshly ground black pepper.

Divide the capsicum slices among the ramekins. Top with the sauce mixture. Place the ramekins in a baking dish and pour enough boiling water into the baking dish to come three-quarters up the side of the ramekins. Transfer to the oven and bake for 60–70 minutes, or until the mixture has set. Remove the ramekins from the oven and leave to stand for 15 minutes.

Meanwhile, make the radicchio and olive salad. Heat 2 tablespoons of the olive oil in a frying pan over medium–high heat. Add the radicchio and cook for 1–2 minutes, or until lightly browned. In a large bowl combine the remaining oil, olives, basil and vinegar. Add the warm radicchio and toss to combine. Arrange on a platter or on individual serving plates.

Turn the sformati out of the ramekins and place on the salad, capsicum side up. Serve immediately.

Similar to a soufflé, though not as airy and far more foolproof, the sformato hails from Italy and is a kind of small savoury flan or pudding made with eggs, seasoning and cheese, cooked in a mould, then turned out to serve.

Haloumi croûtes with onion, raisin and oregano marmalade

1 sourdough baguette, cut into 24 slices,
  each about 5 mm (¼ inch) thick
olive oil, for brushing and pan-frying
200 g (7 oz) haloumi, cut into
  24 small pieces, each about
  5 mm (¼ inch) thick
flour, for dusting
oregano leaves, to garnish

Onion, raisin and oregano marmalade
1½ tablespoons olive oil
2 red onions, thinly sliced
2 teaspoons oregano
30 g (1 oz/¼ cup) dark brown sugar
2 tablespoons white wine
1 tablespoon balsamic vinegar
40 g (1½ oz/⅓ cup) raisins

To make the onion, raisin and oregano marmalade, heat the olive oil in a small heavy-based saucepan over medium heat. Add the onion and cook, stirring, for 8–10 minutes, or until golden and softened. Add the oregano, sugar, wine, vinegar and raisins. Cook over medium–low heat for another 10–15 minutes, or until the marmalade is thick and jammy, stirring occasionally. Remove from the heat and set aside to cool.

Meanwhile, preheat the oven to 180°C (350°F/Gas 4). Arrange the baguette slices on a large baking tray, in a single layer. Brush with olive oil and bake for 8–10 minutes, or until deep golden and crisp.

Heat a generous amount of olive oil in a large frying pan over medium heat. Lightly dust the haloumi in flour, shaking off any excess. Fry the haloumi for 1–2 minutes on each side, or until golden. Drain well on paper towels.

Top each baguette croûte with a piece of haloumi, then some of the marmalade. Garnish with oregano and serve.

Preparation time: 25 minutes   Cooking time: 30 minutes   Makes: 24

Preparation time: 20 minutes
plus 3 hours 15 minutes chilling

Cooking time: 50 minutes

Serves: 4

Chilled Moroccan carrot and capsicum soup

1 tablespoon olive oil
1 large red onion, chopped
3 large red capsicums (peppers), about 600 g (1 lb 5 oz), chopped
2 garlic cloves, sliced
2½ teaspoons ready-made harissa, or to taste
6 carrots (about 1 kg/2 lb 4 oz), chopped
500 ml (17 fl oz/2 cups) vegetable stock
2 tablespoons lemon juice
1 small handful coriander (cilantro) leaves, finely chopped, plus extra leaves, to garnish
ice cubes, to serve
60 g (2¼ oz/⅔ cup) toasted flaked almonds
Turkish bread, to serve

Heat the olive oil in a large saucepan over medium heat. Add the onion and capsicum and cook, stirring, for 10 minutes, or until softened. Add the garlic and harissa and cook for 1 minute, or until aromatic.

Add the carrot, stock and 750 ml (26 fl oz/ 3 cups) water. Bring to the boil, then reduce the heat to low and simmer, uncovered, for 30 minutes or until the carrot is very soft. Remove from the heat and set aside to cool for 15 minutes.

Blend or process the soup until smooth. Transfer to a large bowl, then stir in the lemon juice and coriander. Cover and refrigerate for 3 hours, or until well chilled.

Ladle the soup into serving bowls. Add some ice cubes and serve sprinkled with the flaked almonds and coriander leaves, accompanied by Turkish bread.

Harissa is a hot, spicy chilli paste widely used in North African cooking. It is delicious with tagines and couscous, or can be added to soups, marinades, pasta sauces, casseroles and bean dishes for a flavour hit. You can buy harissa from speciality food stores and some large supermarkets.

Chargrilled vegetable platter with roasted garlic aïoli

Any leftover chargrilled vegetables can be added to a salad or pasta sauce, but they are not suitable for freezing.

The roasted garlic aïoli can be refrigerated in an airtight container for several days.

100 ml (3½ fl oz) extra virgin olive oil
2 tablespoons sea salt
1 teaspoon cracked black pepper
2 tablespoons chopped lemon thyme
2 corn cobs, cut into 5 cm (2 inch) rounds
1 eggplant (aubergine), about 300 g
  (10½ oz), sliced 1 cm (½ inch) thick
2 red onions, peeled leaving the root end
  intact, then each cut into 8 wedges
2 red capsicums (peppers), each cut
  into 6 wedges
2 zucchini (courgettes), cut lengthways
  into 5 mm (¼ inch)-thick slices
2–3 large field mushrooms (about
  200 g/7 oz)
2 bunches asparagus (about 350 g/
  12 oz), trimmed

Roasted garlic aïoli

1 whole garlic bulb
150 ml (5 fl oz) extra virgin olive oil
2 egg yolks
1 tablespoon dijon mustard
125 ml (4 fl oz/½ cup) safflower or
  vegetable oil
1½–2 tablespoons lemon juice

To make the roasted garlic aïoli, preheat the oven to 180°C (350°F/Gas 4). Slice the top from the garlic and place the bulb on a sheet of foil. Drizzle with 2 tablespoons of the olive oil and wrap firmly to enclose. Place on a baking tray and bake for 45 minutes, or until the garlic is tender when pierced with a knife. Remove from the oven and set aside to cool.

Squeeze the pulp out of the cooled garlic, into a food processor. Add the egg yolks and mustard and process until smooth. With the motor running, gradually add the remaining olive oil and the safflower oil in a thin steady stream until the mayonnaise is thick. Stir in lemon juice to taste and season with sea salt and freshly ground black pepper. Cover and refrigerate until about 30 minutes before serving time.

Meanwhile, heat a chargrill pan or barbecue hotplate to medium. In a small bowl, whisk together the olive oil, salt, pepper and lemon thyme. Brush the mixture over the vegetables.

Working in batches as necessary, chargrill the vegetables until charred and tender, using the following times as a guide and removing all the vegetables to a platter as they are cooked. Chargrill the corn, turning occasionally, for 10 minutes; the eggplant and onion for 6–8 minutes, turning once; the capsicum and zucchini for 5–6 minutes, turning once; the mushrooms and asparagus for 5 minutes, turning occasionally.

Serve the vegetables at room temperature with the roasted garlic aïoli.

Preparation time: 20 minutes **Cooking time:** 15 minutes **Makes:** 12

Vegetarian galloping horses

1½ tablespoons peanut oil
8 red Asian shallots (about 200 g/7 oz),
  thinly sliced
1 garlic clove, finely chopped
2 teaspoons finely chopped coriander
  (cilantro) root
1 tablespoon finely grated palm
  sugar (jaggery)
1 tablespoon soy sauce
1 tablespoon lime juice
2 tablespoons finely chopped
  roasted peanuts
½ ripe pineapple (about 875 g/1 lb 15 oz)
1 long red chilli, seeded and cut into long
  thin strips
coriander (cilantro) leaves, to garnish

Heat the oil in a heavy-based frying pan over medium–low heat. Add the shallot, garlic and coriander root and cook, stirring, for 7–10 minutes, or until the shallot softens.

Add the palm sugar and cook, stirring, for 3 minutes. Add the soy sauce and cook for a further 2 minutes, then stir in the lime juice and peanuts. Remove from the heat and set aside to cool. The shallot mixture should be sticky and caramelised.

Cut the skin off the pineapple and remove any eyes. Cut the pineapple into 2 cm (¾ inch)-thick slices and remove the core. Cut the slices into 4 cm (1½ inch) rounds using a pastry cutter.

Arrange the pineapple rounds on a serving platter. Top each with a spoonful of the cooled shallot mixture. Garnish with the chilli and coriander and serve.

This is a delicious version of the dainty Thai appetiser known as 'ma hor', which traditionally uses a spicy stir-fried pork mixture for the topping. By way of inspiration, other fruit such as rambutans, lychees, tangerine or mandarins can also be used for the base, so experiment with your own vegetarian versions. Palm sugar is made from the boiled-down sap of palm trees and ranges in colour from pale golden to deep brown. It is usually hard and dense, and can be found in Asian grocery stores and large supermarkets. This dish is not suitable for freezing.

Cheddar soda bread with pickled cauliflower

Check the bread several times during the baking time. If it appears to be browning too quickly, cover it with foil. It's worth using a good, sharp cheddar in this loaf for the best flavour. The pickled cauliflower will keep in a sealed airtight jar in the refrigerator for up to 10 days.

Cheddar soda bread

200 g (7 oz/1⅓ cups) plain
  (all-purpose) flour
200 g (7 oz/1⅓ cups) wholemeal
  (whole-wheat) flour
2 teaspoons baking powder
1 teaspoon bicarbonate of soda
  (baking soda)
2 teaspoons sea salt
2½ tablespoons caster
  (superfine) sugar
60 g (2¼ oz) butter, chopped
250 g (9 oz/2 cups) grated
  cheddar cheese
350 ml (12 fl oz) buttermilk,
  approximately
cultured butter, to serve

Pickled cauliflower

2½ tablespoons vegetable oil
2 brown onions, cut into 2 cm
  (¾ inch) chunks
2 teaspoons yellow mustard seeds
1 teaspoon cumin seeds
1 teaspoon ground turmeric
1 teaspoon chilli flakes
1 cauliflower (about 700 g/1 lb 9 oz),
  trimmed and cut into small florets
250 ml (9 fl oz/1 cup) white vinegar
110 g (3¾ oz/½ cup) caster
  (superfine) sugar
200 g (7 oz) green beans, trimmed
  and cut into short lengths

Preheat the oven to 180°C (350°F/Gas 4). Lightly grease and flour a baking tray.

To make the cheddar soda bread, sift together the flours, baking powder, bicarbonate of soda and salt into a large bowl, returning any wholemeal flour solids to the mixture. Stir in the sugar, then rub in the butter until evenly incorporated. Stir in the cheddar, then pour in the buttermilk and stir with a flat-bladed knife until a soft dough forms; it might be necessary to add a little more buttermilk to bring the mixture together. Turn out onto a floured surface and briefly knead until smooth. Shape into a round loaf about 20 cm (8 inches) in diameter. Using a large sharp knife, slash a deep cross in the top of the loaf.

Bake the bread for 50 minutes, or until cooked through and crusty; the loaf should sound hollow when tapped on the base. Transfer to a wire rack to cool.

While the loaf is baking, prepare the pickled cauliflower. Heat the oil in a large saucepan over medium heat. Add the onion and cook, stirring, for 2–3 minutes, or until softened slightly. Add the spices and cook for 2 minutes, or until aromatic, stirring often. Add the cauliflower and toss to coat well, then add the vinegar, sugar and 125 ml (4 fl oz/½ cup) water, stirring to dissolve the sugar. Bring to a simmer, then cover and cook over medium heat for 2 minutes. Add the beans and cook, covered, for a final 2 minutes. Remove the pan from the heat. Keeping the lid on, set aside until the mixture is cool.

Slice the loaf using a serrated knife. Serve with butter and the pickled cauliflower.

Preparation time: 30 minutes   **Cooking time:** 50 minutes   **Serves:** 6

Preparation time: 15 minutes   **Cooking time:** 15 minutes   **Serves:** 4

Asparagus and snow pea tempura

8 thin asparagus spears
20 snow peas (mangetout)
plain (all-purpose) flour, for dusting
vegetable oil, for deep-frying

Soy ginger dipping sauce
125 ml (4 fl oz/½ cup) light soy sauce
1 tablespoon finely shredded
   fresh ginger

Batter
1 egg yolk
250 ml (9 fl oz/1 cup) chilled
   sparkling mineral water
150 g (5½ oz/1 cup) plain
   (all-purpose) flour

In a small serving bowl, mix together the soy ginger dipping sauce ingredients. Set aside.

Trim the asparagus spears and halve them. Top the snow peas and remove the strings.

Line a plate with paper towels. Place some flour in a bowl for dusting the vegetables. Toss the asparagus and snow peas in the flour and dust off any excess.

In a deep-fryer or wok, heat 5 cm (2 inches) oil over medium–high heat.

While the oil is heating, and working quickly, make the batter. Lightly beat the egg yolk in a bowl with a pair of chopsticks. Pour in the mineral water and quickly stir to combine. Now add the flour and stir until just combined to form a slightly lumpy batter — don't worry about a few undissolved flour lumps.

Drop a little batter into the hot oil. If the batter rises, surrounded by tiny bubbles, the oil is ready.

Working in batches, dip each vegetable piece into the batter, gently shaking off the excess. Slide the vegetables into the hot oil and fry for 2–3 minutes, or until lightly golden. Drain on paper towels while repeating with the remaining vegetables.

Serve immediately, with the dipping sauce.

Light soy sauce has not been aged as long as regular soy sauce. It is lighter in colour and has a thinner viscosity but is saltier. You'll find it in Asian grocery stores and larger supermarkets.

Mushroom caviar with olive bread

Any variety of mushrooms can be used in this mushroom caviar – try a combination of button, Swiss brown, oyster, field, shiitake and/or pine mushrooms. You could also use just one variety on its own, if you like.

Olive bread

375 g (13 oz/2½ cups) plain (all-purpose) flour, approximately

2 teaspoons dried yeast

2 teaspoons caster (superfine) sugar

1 teaspoon sea salt

160 g (5¾ oz/1 cup) pitted kalamata olives, coarsely chopped

2 teaspoons milk

Mushroom caviar

20 g (¾ oz) butter

400 g (14 oz/4 cups) finely chopped mixed mushrooms

1 garlic clove, crushed

1 teaspoon sea salt

2 tablespoons lemon juice

2 tablespoons sour cream

1 tablespoon finely chopped flat-leaf (Italian) parsley

To make the olive bread, combine the flour, yeast, sugar and salt in a large bowl. Make a well in the centre. Add 250 ml (9 fl oz/1 cup) lukewarm water and using a wooden spoon and then your hands, mix to form a dough. Turn out onto a lightly floured surface and knead for 10 minutes, or until smooth and elastic, gradually adding a little extra flour if the dough remains sticky. Place the dough in a lightly oiled bowl, turning to coat in the oil. Cover with plastic wrap and stand in a warm, draught-free place for 1 hour, or until doubled in size.

Preheat the oven to 180°C (350°F/Gas 4). Grease a large baking tray.

Pat the olives dry using paper towels. Knock down the dough and turn out onto a lightly floured surface. Knead briefly, then roll out to a large round. Sprinkle the olives in the centre, then fold in the dough to enclose them and shape it into a 20 cm (8 inch) round. Place on the baking tray and brush with the milk. Bake for 35–40 minutes, or until the loaf is golden brown and sounds hollow when tapped on the base. Remove from the oven and leave on the tray for 5 minutes, then transfer to a wire rack to cool.

Meanwhile, make the mushroom caviar. Melt the butter in a large frying pan over medium heat. Add the mushroom and garlic and cook, stirring, for 3–4 minutes. Sprinkle with the salt and lemon juice and cook for a further 2–3 minutes, or until the mushrooms have softened. Season to taste with sea salt and freshly ground black pepper.

Remove the mushrooms from the heat and allow to cool for 10 minutes. Transfer to a serving bowl. Stir in the sour cream and parsley and serve with slices of olive bread.

Preparation time: 20 minutes
plus 1 hour proving

Cooking time: 40 minutes

Serves: 4–6

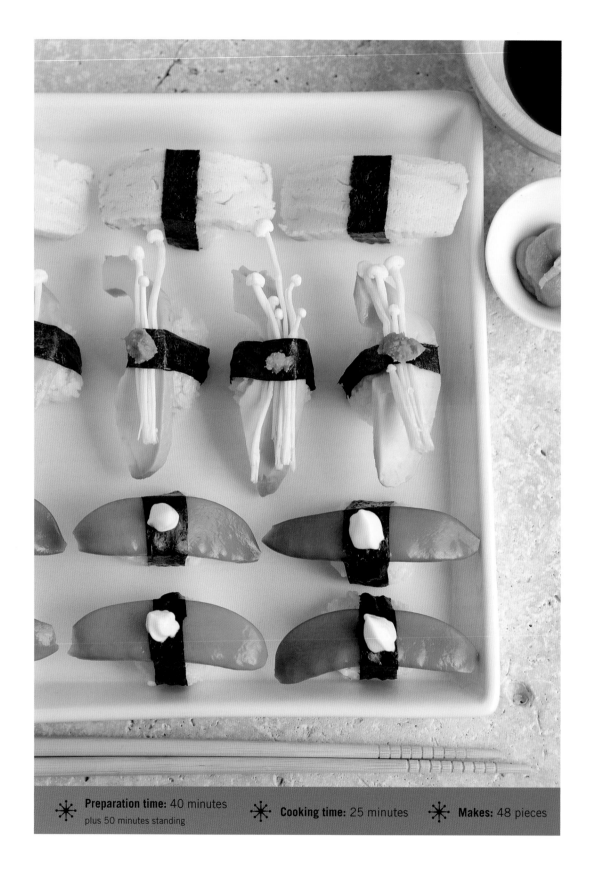

Preparation time: 40 minutes plus 50 minutes standing

Cooking time: 25 minutes

Makes: 48 pieces

Vegetarian sushi

660 g (1 lb 7 oz/3 cups) sushi rice
4 cm (1½ inch) square of kombu
60 ml (2 fl oz/¼ cup) sake
80 ml (2½ fl oz/⅓ cup) rice wine vinegar
1 tablespoon caster (superfine) sugar
¾ teaspoon sea salt flakes
4 nori sheets, cut into 12 x 1.5 cm
 (4½ x ⅝ inch) strips
sushi soy sauce, to serve
wasabi, to serve
pickled ginger, to serve

Omelette topping
5 eggs, lightly beaten
2 teaspoons mirin
3 teaspoons vegetable oil

Avocado topping
1 firm, ripe avocado, halved, stoned,
 peeled and cut lengthways into 16 slices,
 each about 5 mm (¼ inch) thick
50 g (1¾ oz) enoki mushrooms, trimmed
 and separated into small clumps
1½ teaspoons red miso paste

Snow pea topping
100 g (3½ oz/1 cup) snow peas
 (mangetout), trimmed and blanched
 in boiling water for 15 seconds
3 teaspoons Japanese mayonnaise

Rinse the rice in a sieve until the water runs clear. Drain the rice for 30 minutes, then place in a saucepan with the kombu and 750 ml (26 fl oz/ 3 cups) water. Bring to the boil over high heat, reduce the heat to very low, then cover and simmer gently for 13 minutes or until tender. Remove from the heat, sprinkle with the sake, re-cover and stand for 10 minutes.

Put the rice in a shallow dish and remove the kombu. Swirl the vinegar, sugar and salt in a small saucepan over medium–low heat to dissolve the sugar and salt. Using a wooden spoon, gently fold the vinegar mixture through the rice. Set aside for 15 minutes, or until the rice has cooled.

To make the omelette, whisk together the eggs and mirin. Heat the oil in a large non-stick frying pan over medium–low heat. Pour in egg mixture and cook for 3–4 minutes or until almost set. Cover the pan with a plate and turn out the omelette. Carefully slide back into pan and cook for another 2–3 minutes or until just set. Carefully slide onto a chopping board and cut into 2 cm (¾ inch) strips with a hot, wet knife. Cut strips into rectangles 6 cm (2½ inches) long. Set aside.

To make the sushi, use wet hands to scoop out a heaped tablespoon of rice with your left hand. Curl the fingers of your left hand around the rice and place your thumb over the end to form a rice cushion. Place the first two fingers of your right hand along the rice and squeeze gently with both hands to pack the rice into a rounded mound 2 cm (¾ inch) wide, 5 cm (2 inches) long and 2.5 cm (1 inch) high. Repeat to make 48 mounds.

Top 16 rice mounds with avocado and enoki mushrooms. Wrap a nori strip around the centre of each one, securing it underneath. Place a dab of miso paste on top. Top 16 rice mounds with a snow pea; fix each with a nori strip and a dab of mayonnaise. Top remaining mounds with omelette strips and fasten with strips of nori.

Serve with little bowls of soy sauce, wasabi and pickled ginger.

You'll find all the sushi ingredients in an Asian supermarket.
Kombu is a type of dried seaweed that is cooked with the sushi rice to subtly season it.
Nori sheets are paper-thin squares of pressed dried seaweed sheets.
Japanese mayonnaise has a thinner texture than Western mayonnaise and slightly different flavour. It is often sold in plastic squeeze bottles.

Chilled tomato mousse with sesame pastries

Semi-dried tomatoes aren't as dry and chewy as sun-dried tomatoes and have a softer texture and flavour. They are sold in jars in supermarkets, and loose at the deli counter.

150 g (5½ oz/1 cup) chopped semi-dried
  (sun-blushed) tomatoes
1 teaspoon tomato paste
  (concentrated purée)
1 small handful basil leaves
1 teaspoon caster (superfine) sugar
¼ teaspoon Tabasco sauce, or to taste
60 g (2¼ oz/¼ cup) sour cream
60 ml (2 fl oz/¼ cup) thickened cream
½ teaspoon powdered gelatine
60 ml (2 fl oz/¼ cup) tomato juice

Sesame pastries

150 g (5½ oz/1 cup) plain
  (all-purpose) flour
50 g (1¾ oz) chilled butter, chopped
35 g (1¼ oz/⅓ cup) finely grated
  parmesan cheese, plus extra,
  for sprinkling
2 egg yolks
½ teaspoon freshly cracked black pepper
1 tablespoon sesame seeds

Place the tomatoes, tomato paste, basil, sugar, Tabasco sauce and 1 tablespoon water in a small food processor and blend until smooth. Transfer to a bowl, then stir in the sour cream.

Whisk the cream in a bowl until soft peaks form. Fold the cream into the tomato mixture, then spoon the mousse into four 125 ml (4 fl oz/ ½ cup) glasses.

Combine the gelatine and 2 tablespoons boiling water in a small cup, stirring until the gelatine has dissolved. Stir in the tomato juice, then carefully pour the mixture over the top of each mousse. Cover and refrigerate for 3 hours, or overnight.

To make the sesame pastries, preheat the oven to 180°C (350°F/Gas 4). Line two baking trays with baking paper. Place the flour in a bowl, then rub in the butter until the mixture resembles breadcrumbs. Stir in the parmesan. Add one of the egg yolks, the pepper, sesame seeds and about 1 tablespoon cold water, or enough to form a firm dough. Knead lightly to bring the pastry together, then wrap in plastic wrap and refrigerate for 30 minutes.

Roll the pastry out to about 2.5 mm (⅛ inch) thick, then cut out rounds using a 5 cm (2 inch) pastry cutter. Place on the baking trays.

In a small bowl, whisk the remaining egg yolk with 2 teaspoons water. Brush the mixture lightly over the biscuits and sprinkle each with a little extra parmesan. Bake for 15 minutes, or until golden. Cool on a wire rack, then serve with the tomato mousse.

Preparation time: 30 minutes
plus 3 hours chilling

Cooking time: 15 minutes

Serves: 4

Preparation time: 35 minutes
plus 30 minutes soaking

Cooking time:
1 hour 50 minutes

Makes: 18

44   VEGETARIAN

Split pea samosas

6 sheets frozen shortcrust pastry, thawed
1 egg, lightly beaten
plain yoghurt, to serve
mango chutney or lime pickle, to serve

Filling
330 g (11½ oz/1½ cups) dried yellow
  split peas
80 ml (2½ fl oz/⅓ cup) peanut oil
2 small brown onions, thinly sliced
4 garlic cloves, thinly sliced
2 long green chillies, finely chopped
1½ tablespoons grated fresh ginger
½ teaspoon freshly ground black pepper
1 teaspoon ground turmeric
2 teaspoons cumin seeds
10 curry leaves
2 teaspoons black mustard seeds
2 teaspoons sea salt flakes
2 tablespoons lemon juice
1 large handful coriander (cilantro) leaves,
  coarsely chopped

To make the filling, wash the split peas well, then place in a bowl. Cover with cold water and leave to soak for 30 minutes.

Meanwhile, heat 60 ml (2 fl oz/¼ cup) of the oil in a large saucepan over medium–high heat. Add the onion and cook, stirring occasionally, for 10 minutes, or until golden. Reduce the heat to medium–low and cook for a further 6–8 minutes, or until the onion is soft and deep golden. Add the garlic, chilli, ginger, pepper, turmeric and cumin seeds, then cook, stirring, for 2 minutes, or until aromatic.

Drain the split peas and add them to the pan. Pour in 1.5 litres (52 fl oz/6 cups) water, cover and bring to a simmer. Cook for 30 minutes, stirring occasionally. Remove the lid and cook for a further 30 minutes, stirring often, until the mixture is a thick porridge-like consistency.

Heat the remaining oil in a small frying pan. Add the curry leaves and mustard seeds and fry until the seeds start to pop and the leaves are crisp. Stir into the split pea mixture with the salt, lemon juice and coriander. Remove from the heat and set aside to cool to room temperature. Remove the curry leaves from the mixture.

Preheat the oven to 200°C (400°F/Gas 6). Line a baking tray with baking paper.

Cut the pastry into 18 rounds using a 13 cm (5 inch) pastry cutter. Brush the edges with beaten egg, then place 1½ tablespoons of the filling on one half of each round. Fold the pastry over the filling to form a half-moon shape, then press or crimp the edges together to seal well.

Place the samosas on the lined tray and brush the tops with a little of the remaining beaten egg. Bake for 20–25 minutes, or until the pastry is golden and cooked through.

Serve the samosas with yoghurt and some mango chutney or lime pickle.

From a tree native to Asia, small, shiny curry leaves impart a spicy curry flavour to dishes. They are available both fresh and dried from Asian grocery stores and large supermarkets; buy fresh leaves where possible as they are more aromatic. They are not edible, so remove them from dishes before serving.
Yellow split peas are sold in packets in supermarkets.

Mini pumpkin pancakes with slow-roasted tomatoes and creamy pesto

These pancakes are bite sized and deliciously moist. When you are cooking these pancakes, bubbles will not appear across the surface, so you will need to judge the cooking time by the colour of the pancake.

30 cherry tomatoes (about 250 g/9 oz), halved
1½ tablespoons olive oil, plus extra, for pan-frying
1 tablespoon balsamic vinegar
2 teaspoons caster (superfine) sugar
small basil leaves, to garnish

Mini pumpkin pancakes
250 g (9 oz/2 cups) coarsely grated pumpkin (winter squash)
60 ml (2 fl oz/¼ cup) milk, approximately
75 g (2½ oz/½ cup) plain (all-purpose) flour
½ teaspoon baking powder
2 eggs, lightly beaten

Creamy pesto
125 g (4½ oz/½ cup) ready-made basil pesto
60 g (2¼ oz/¼ cup) crème fraîche or sour cream

Preheat the oven to 120ºC (235ºF/Gas ½).

Place the tomatoes on a baking tray lined with baking paper, cut side up. Drizzle with the olive oil and vinegar, then sprinkle with the sugar. Season to taste with sea salt and freshly ground black pepper. Roast for 1½ hours, then remove from the oven.

To make the mini pumpkin pancakes, place the pumpkin and milk in a small saucepan over medium heat. Bring to a simmer, then reduce the heat to low, cover and cook, stirring occasionally, for 8 minutes, or until the pumpkin is very soft. Remove from the heat and mash the pumpkin with a fork. Set aside to cool to room temperature.

Sift the flour and baking powder into a bowl. Combine the pumpkin mixture and eggs and use a balloon whisk to stir into the flour to make a smooth batter, about the consistency of soft whipped cream; if necessary, add a little extra milk, a tablespoon at a time. Season to taste.

Heat a large non-stick frying pan over medium heat. Lightly oil the pan just to grease the surface. Place heaped teaspoonfuls of the batter into the frying pan to make pancakes about 4 cm (1½ inches) in diameter. Cook on each side for 2 minutes, or until light golden brown. Cook the pancakes in batches, brushing the pan with oil between each batch. Transfer the pancakes to a plate and keep warm while cooking the remaining batter.

Combine the creamy pesto ingredients in a bowl and stir until smooth.

Serve the pancakes topped with 2 roasted tomato halves, a spoonful of creamy pesto and 1–2 basil leaves.

| ✳ **Preparation time:** 30 minutes | ✳ **Cooking time:**
1 hour 30 minutes | ✳ **Makes:** about 30 |

Preparation time: 15 minutes   **Cooking time:** 45 minutes   **Serves:** 4–6

Roast parsnip, pumpkin, chestnut and pear salad

3 parsnips (about 450 g/1 lb)
2 beurre bosc pears
8 thyme sprigs
1 tablespoon honey
80 ml (2½ fl oz/⅓ cup) olive oil
500 g (1 lb 2 oz) jap or butternut
  pumpkin (squash)
400 g (14 oz) fresh chestnuts, peeled,
  or 200 g (7 oz) frozen peeled
  chestnuts, thawed
100 g (3½ oz) rocket (arugula)

Orange and sherry vinegar dressing
80 ml (2½ fl oz/⅓ cup) extra virgin
  olive oil
1½ tablespoons sherry vinegar
1 teaspoon finely grated orange rind
1 garlic clove, crushed

Preheat the oven to 180°C (350°F/Gas 4).

Peel and trim the parsnips, then trim tips. Cut the parsnips into quarters lengthways and place in a large roasting tin. Cut the pears in half down the middle, remove the core, then cut each half into three wedges. Place in the roasting tin with the parsnip. Scatter with half the thyme sprigs, then drizzle with half the honey and 2½ tablespoons of the olive oil. Season to taste with sea salt and freshly ground black pepper.

Peel the pumpkin, remove the seeds, then cut the flesh into 1 cm (½ inch)-thick slices. Place in another roasting tin, scatter with the remaining thyme sprigs and drizzle with the remaining honey and oil. Season to taste.

Bake the parsnip, pear and pumpkin for 20 minutes. Turn them over and roast for a further 10 minutes, or until the pumpkin is tender. Remove the pumpkin from the oven.

Add the chestnuts to the parsnip and pear and roast for a further 15 minutes, or until all are tender and golden. Remove from the oven and allow to cool slightly.

Meanwhile, place the orange and sherry vinegar dressing ingredients in a small bowl and whisk together well.

In a large mixing bowl, combine the pumpkin, parsnip, pear, chestnuts and rocket. Drizzle the dressing over and toss gently to combine.

Arrange on a platter, or divide among serving bowls or plates and serve.

Beurre bosc pears have a bronze, deep golden or russeted skin and an elegant, elongated shape. The flesh is sweet and creamy, with a slightly grainy texture. They are a great cooking pear as they hold their shape well.

To peel fresh chestnuts, cut a cross into the flat side of each chestnut using a small sharp knife. Place them on a baking tray and roast in a preheated 200°C (400°F/Gas 6) oven for 10–20 minutes, or until the outer shell starts to peel away. Remove from the oven and allow to cool, then peel the shell and skin away.

Roast tomato, sweet potato and orange soup with basil oil

This soup can be frozen in an airtight container for up to 6 weeks.

1.5 kg (3 lb 5 oz) sweet potato, peeled and cut into 3 cm (1¼ inch) chunks
2 tablespoons thyme leaves, plus extra, to garnish
100 ml (3½ fl oz) olive oil
4 vine-ripened tomatoes (about 550 g/ 1 lb 4 oz), chopped
3 garlic cloves, chopped
1 tablespoon chopped sage, plus extra sage leaves, to garnish
2 teaspoons balsamic vinegar
2 brown onions, thinly sliced
2 carrots, cut into 1 cm (½ inch) chunks
2 celery stalks, thinly sliced
2.5 litres (87 fl oz/10 cups) vegetable stock
60 ml (2 fl oz/¼ cup) freshly squeezed orange juice

Basil oil
2 large handfuls basil leaves
125 ml (4 fl oz/½ cup) extra virgin olive oil

Preheat the oven to 180°C (350°F/Gas 4). Line two baking trays with baking paper.

Place the sweet potato on one baking tray. Sprinkle with half the thyme and drizzle with 2 tablespoons of the olive oil. Season to taste with sea salt and freshly ground black pepper and toss to coat.

Place the tomato, garlic and sage on the other baking tray. Drizzle with the vinegar and 1 tablespoon of the olive oil. Season to taste and toss to coat.

Roast the sweet potato and tomato, swapping the trays halfway through cooking, for 35 minutes, or until the sweet potato is tender and golden and the tomato is just collapsing. Remove from the oven and set aside.

Heat the remaining oil in a large saucepan over medium–low heat. Add the onion, carrot, celery and remaining thyme. Cook, stirring, for 10–15 minutes, or until the vegetables start to soften. Pour in the stock and orange juice, then add the roasted sweet potato, tomato and any cooking juices. Simmer, uncovered, for 25 minutes, or until the vegetables are tender. Remove from the heat and allow to cool slightly.

Meanwhile, to make the basil oil, place the basil and olive oil in a food processor and blend until combined.

Transfer the soup in batches to a food processor and process until smooth. Return the soup to the saucepan and bring to a simmer. Season to taste.

Ladle the soup into serving bowls and drizzle with the basil oil. Garnish with extra thyme and sage, and serve.

Braised beetroot salad with goat's cheese croûtes

4 beetroot (beets) (about 750 g/
  1 lb 10 oz), with stems and leaves
250 ml (9 fl oz/1 cup) red wine
500 ml (17 fl oz/2 cups) vegetable stock
80 ml (2½ fl oz/⅓ cup) red wine vinegar
2 tablespoons caster (superfine) sugar
1½ tablespoons olive oil
1 garlic clove, crushed
2 teaspoons oregano leaves, chopped
1 small (25 cm/10 inch) baguette,
  cut into 12 slices, each about 5 mm
  (¼ inch) thick
80 g (2¾ oz/⅔ cup) crumbled goat's
  cheese
¼ cup flat-leaf (Italian) parsley leaves

Raisin dressing
2 teaspoons soft brown sugar
2 tablespoons red wine vinegar
1 teaspoon dijon mustard
40 g (1½ oz/¼ cup) finely chopped raisins
60 ml (2 fl oz/¼ cup) extra virgin olive oil

To make the raisin dressing, place the sugar, vinegar and 125 ml (4 fl oz/½ cup) water in a small saucepan. Stir over medium heat until the sugar has dissolved. Add the mustard and raisins and simmer for 5 minutes. Remove from the heat and leave to stand for 30 minutes. Whisk in the olive oil and season to taste with sea salt and freshly ground black pepper.

Trim the beetroot, reserving the stems and leaves. Wash the beetroot bulbs, then peel and cut them into 2.5 cm (1 inch) wedges and place in a medium saucepan. Pour in the wine, stock and 2 tablespoons of the vinegar, then stir in the sugar. Bring to the boil over medium heat, then cover and simmer for 20 minutes.

Wash and dry the reserved beetroot stems and leaves. Reserving the leaves, cut the stems into 5 cm (2 inch) lengths, then add to the beetroot wedges in the pan. Cover and simmer for a further 15 minutes, or until the wedges are tender. Add the reserved leaves, then cover and cook for a further 4–5 minutes, or until the leaves are tender. Remove from the heat and set aside to cool. Drain well and transfer to a large bowl.

Meanwhile, preheat the oven to 180°C (350°F/Gas 4). Combine the olive oil, garlic and oregano in a small bowl. Brush the mixture over one side of the baguette slices and arrange on a baking tray. Spread with the goat's cheese and bake for 5–8 minutes, or until golden and crisp.

Drizzle the raisin dressing over the beetroot and add the parsley. Toss to combine and season to taste. Serve with the croutons.

Broad bean and haloumi fritters with walnut tarator

Turkish in origin, tarator is a thick, garlicky walnut sauce that is often served with cooked vegetables. Ideally it should be made several hours ahead to allow the flavours to blend together.

To toast walnuts, dry-fry them in a frying pan over medium heat for 2–3 minutes, or until aromatic, tossing often so they don't burn. Tip them into a bowl to cool.

1 desiree potato (about 120 g/4 oz)
400 g (14 oz/2½ cups) frozen broad (fava) beans
1 egg, lightly beaten
1 small handful dill sprigs, plus extra, to garnish
1 small handful mint leaves, plus extra, to garnish
1 teaspoon finely grated lemon rind
1 tablespoon lemon juice
1 teaspoon ground cumin
¼ teaspoon chilli powder
150 g (5½ oz) haloumi cheese, coarsely grated
2 teaspoons plain (all-purpose) flour
vegetable oil for pan-frying

Walnut tarator
2 slices day-old white bread, crusts removed
60 g (2¼ oz/½ cup) walnut pieces, lightly toasted
2 garlic cloves, crushed
1 teaspoon sea salt
2 teaspoons red wine vinegar, or to taste
2 tablespoons olive oil
250 g (9 oz/1 cup) Greek-style yoghurt

To make the walnut tarator, place the bread, walnuts, garlic, salt, vinegar and olive oil in a food processor. Blend until a coarse paste forms, then transfer to a bowl and stir in the yoghurt. Stir in 1–2 tablespoons warm water to loosen the sauce. Cover and refrigerate for 2 hours.

Cook the whole potato in a saucepan of boiling water for 20 minutes or until very tender when tested with a skewer. Drain. When cool enough to handle, peel away the skin, then mash the flesh with a fork until smooth. Set aside.

Cook the broad beans in a saucepan of boiling water for 2 minutes, or until tender. Drain and leave until cool enough to handle, then peel.

Place the broad beans in a food processor with the egg, dill, mint, lemon rind, lemon juice, cumin and chilli powder. Blend just until a coarse paste forms — do not overprocess as the mixture should still be a little chunky. Transfer to a bowl, then stir through the mashed potato, haloumi and flour.

Pour enough oil into a large frying pan just to cover the base and place over medium heat. When the oil is hot, drop tablespoons of the mixture into it, flattening each one slightly. Cook the fritters in batches for 2 minutes on each side, or until deep golden and heated through — take care not to overcook them or the fritters will burn. Drain on paper towels while cooking the remaining fritters.

Serve the fritters garnished with extra dill and mint, and accompanied by the walnut tarator.

Preparation time: 20 minutes
plus 2 hours standing

Cooking time: 45 minutes

Serves: 4
(makes 20)

Preparation time: 5 minutes
plus 15 minutes soaking

Cooking time: 10 minutes

Serves: 4

Miso broth with tofu and mushrooms

5 g (⅛ oz) shredded wakame
1 litre (35 fl oz/4 cups) vegetable stock
2 tablespoons white miso paste
2 baby bok choy (pak choy), finely
   shredded
1 teaspoon finely grated fresh ginger
1 tablespoon mirin
100 g (3½ oz) enoki mushrooms,
   separated into small bunches
80 g (2¾ oz/1¾ cups) baby English
   spinach leaves
300 g (10½ oz) silken tofu, drained and
   cut into 1 cm (½ inch) cubes
1 spring onion (scallion), diagonally sliced

Soak the wakame in warm water for 15 minutes, or until rehydrated. Drain and cut into 2 cm (¾ inch) lengths.

Pour the stock and 250 ml (9 fl oz/1 cup) cold water into a large saucepan. Bring to the boil over high heat, then reduce the heat to low. Add the wakame and miso paste and stir until well combined.

Add the bok choy and cook over low heat for 1–2 minutes. Stir in the ginger, mirin and mushrooms and remove the pan from the heat.

Divide the spinach and tofu among serving bowls. Ladle the soup over the top, garnish with the spring onion and serve.

Wakame is a type of dried seaweed. Its flavour enhances soups such as this one, but it needs to be soaked in water before using to soften it.
White miso paste, which is actually pale yellow in colour, is the fermented paste of soya beans, salt and either rice or barley. It has a sweet, mellow taste and relatively low salt content. You'll find wakame and white miso paste in health food and Asian grocery stores.
Enoki mushrooms are pale, delicate mushrooms with long, thin stalks and tiny caps. They are very fragile and need minimal cooking.

Quinoa and vegetable soup

Pronounced 'keen-wah', quinoa is a grain native to South America. It has the highest protein content of any grain and contains B vitamins, calcium and vitamin E. Quinoa makes a great base for salads and soups, and is an ideal substitute for brown rice, having a similar nutty flavour. When cooked it becomes translucent, with its 'germ ring' visible. It is available from health food stores.

2 tablespoons olive oil
1 large brown onion, finely chopped
2 carrots, finely chopped
2 celery stalks, finely chopped
2 garlic cloves, crushed
2 thyme sprigs
1 tablespoon ground fennel seeds
2 teaspoons ground cumin
1 teaspoon ground turmeric
750 ml (26 fl oz/3 cups) vegetable stock
500 g (1 lb 2 oz/2½ cups) chopped
    vine-ripened tomatoes
100 g (3½ oz/½ cup) quinoa
400 g (14 oz) tin chickpeas, rinsed
    and drained
¼ cup finely chopped flat-leaf (Italian)
    parsley leaves
60 g (2 oz/¼ cup) Greek-style yoghurt
lemon or lime wedges, to serve (optional)

Heat the olive oil in a saucepan over medium–high heat. Add the onion, carrot and celery. Cook, stirring, for 10 minutes, or until the vegetables start to soften. Add the garlic, thyme sprigs, ground fennel, cumin and turmeric. Cook, stirring, for 1 minute, or until aromatic.

Add the stock, tomatoes and 500 ml (17 fl oz/2 cups) water. Bring to the boil, then reduce the heat to low and simmer, uncovered, for 30 minutes.

Meanwhile, cook the quinoa in a small saucepan of boiling water for 10 minutes, or until tender. Drain.

Stir the quinoa, chickpeas and parsley into the soup and heat through.

Ladle the soup into serving bowls. Serve with a dollop of yoghurt, and lemon or lime wedges if desired.

Middle Eastern burghul salad

125 g (4½ oz/⅔ cup) fine burghul
  (bulgur)
60 ml (2 fl oz/¼ cup) lemon juice
70 g (2½ oz/½ cup) pistachio nuts
125 g (4½ oz) baby green beans,
  trimmed
1 small red onion, finely chopped
40 g (1½ oz/⅓ cup) dried cranberries
2 large handfuls flat-leaf (Italian) parsley,
  finely chopped
1 handful mint, finely chopped
1 tablespoon pomegranate molasses
1 teaspoon sugar
2 tablespoons olive oil
12 baby cos (romaine) lettuce leaves
  (about 2 heads of baby cos lettuce)
pitta bread, toasted, to serve

Place the burghul in a small bowl. Stir in the lemon juice and 125 ml (4 fl oz/½ cup) warm water. Leave to soak for 30 minutes, or until the burghul is tender.

Preheat the oven to 150°C (300°F/Gas 2). Place the pistachios on a baking tray and roast for 10–12 minutes. Allow to cool slightly, then coarsely chop.

Meanwhile, cook the beans in a saucepan of boiling water for 3 minutes, or until tender-crisp and bright green. Drain and refresh under cold running water until cooled. Drain and slice thinly, then set aside.

Place the burghul, pistachios, beans, onion, cranberries and herbs in a large bowl. Mix together the pomegranate molasses, sugar and olive oil, then drizzle over the burghul mixture and toss gently to combine.

Arrange three lettuce leaves on each serving plate. Divide the burghul mixture among the leaves and serve with pitta bread.

Also known as cracked wheat, burghul is the key ingredient in tabouleh. You can buy it whole, or cracked into fine, medium or coarse grains. Being pre-steamed and pre-baked, burghul requires little or no cooking, but is usually soaked before using to soften it. Pomegranate molasses is the boiled-down juice of a sour variety of pomegranate. It has an unusual bitter-sweet flavour and is used in sauces and dressings. It is available from Middle Eastern grocery stores.

Soba noodle salad with tofu, radish and sesame

A speciality of northern Japan, soba noodles are thin, beige-coloured noodles made from buckwheat (and sometimes wheat) flour. They are usually sold dried; some are lightly flavoured with green tea or beetroot (beets). You'll find them in large supermarkets, health food stores and Asian grocery stores.

90 g (3¼ oz) dried soba noodles
2 tablespoons sesame seeds
250 ml (9 fl oz/1 cup) peanut oil
300 g (10½ oz) firm tofu, drained and
 cut into 2 cm (¾ inch) cubes
2 tablespoons cornflour (cornstarch)
3 radishes (about 300 g/10½ oz),
 trimmed and thinly sliced
100 g (3½ oz) snow pea (mangetout)
 sprouts, halved
1 handful coriander (cilantro) leaves
4 spring onions (scallions), thinly sliced
 on the diagonal

Wasabi miso dressing
1½ tablespoons white miso paste
2 tablespoons rice wine vinegar
½ teaspoon wasabi
2 teaspoons tamari
60 ml (2 fl oz/¼ cup) rice bran oil

To make the wasabi miso dressing, whisk the miso paste, vinegar, wasabi and tamari in a small bowl to combine. Slowly whisk in the oil, then season to taste with sea salt and freshly ground black pepper. Set aside.

Bring a large saucepan of water to the boil. Add the noodles and cook for 4 minutes, or until tender. Drain, rinse with cold water and drain again.

Meanwhile, dry-roast the sesame seeds in a large frying pan over medium–low heat for 2 minutes, or until golden all over, stirring occasionally. Remove to a plate.

Add the peanut oil to the pan. Heat the oil over medium–high heat until hot. Dust the tofu with the cornflour and fry for 2 minutes on each side, or until golden all over. Drain on paper towels.

Place the noodles, sesame seeds and warm tofu in a large bowl with the radish, snow pea sprouts and dressing. Season to taste and gently toss to combine.

Divide among serving bowls and serve sprinkled with the coriander and spring onion.

Preparation time: 30 minutes
plus overnight soaking

Cooking time: 35 minutes

Serves: 6

Banh xeo

110 g (3¾ oz/½ cup) dried split mung
 beans, soaked overnight
2 tablespoons peanut oil
250 g (9 oz) mixed Asian mushrooms
 such as shiitake, shimeji, king and enoki,
 coarsely chopped
90 g (3¼ oz/1 cup) bean sprouts,
 tails trimmed
2 garlic cloves, finely chopped
5 snake (yard long) beans, cut into 4 cm
 (1½ inch) lengths
1 butter lettuce, leaves separated,
 washed and spun dry
1 handful mint leaves
1 handful Thai basil leaves

Lime chilli dressing
45 g (1½ oz/⅓ cup) finely grated palm
 sugar (jaggery)
2 tablespoons lime juice
2 tablespoons light soy sauce
¼ bird's eye chilli, finely diced

Pancake batter
225 g (8 oz/1¼ cups) rice flour
2 teaspoons ground turmeric
½ teaspoon sea salt flakes
375 ml (13 fl oz/1½ cups) chilled
 sparkling mineral water
270 ml (9½ fl oz) coconut milk
3 spring onions (scallions), thinly sliced

To make the lime chilli dressing, put the palm
sugar and 125 ml (4 fl oz/½ cup) water in a
small saucepan and stir over medium heat until
the sugar has dissolved. Leave to cool, then stir
in the lime juice, soy sauce and chilli. Set aside.

Line a steamer or bamboo basket with muslin
(cheesecloth). Drain the soaked mung beans and
place in the steamer or bamboo basket. Place
over a saucepan of boiling water. Cover and cook
for 15 minutes, or until just tender. Remove from
the heat and set aside.

Heat the oil in a large non-stick frying
pan over high heat until very hot. Add all the
mushrooms (except any enoki) and stir-fry for
3 minutes, or until golden brown. Add any enoki
mushrooms, along with the bean sprouts, garlic
and snake beans. Stir-fry for another minute,
then season to taste with sea salt and freshly
ground black pepper. Transfer the mixture to
a bowl and wipe the pan clean.

To make the pancake batter, combine the rice
flour, turmeric and salt in a bowl, then mix in
the mineral water, coconut milk and spring onion
until smooth.

Place the frying pan back over medium heat.
Add one-quarter of the pancake mixture and
swirl to coat the base. Sprinkle one-quarter of
the steamed mung beans and one-quarter of the
mushroom mixture over one half of the pancake.
Cook for 3 minutes, or until deep golden brown,
crisp underneath and just cooked through. Fold
the other side of the pancake over the filling,
then slip the pancake out of the frying pan and
cut into four pieces.

Repeat with the remaining pancake batter
and filling to make another three pancakes.

Divide the lettuce leaves and herbs among
serving plates. Top with pancake pieces and serve
drizzled with the lime chilli dressing.

In Vietnam, these savoury pancakes
(pronounced 'bahn say-oh') are a
popular street snack. Their name
translates roughly as 'sizzling crepe',
which refers to the sizzle of the batter
as it hits the hot pan. Surprisingly
the batter is made without eggs, with
turmeric being responsible for its
golden colour. The filling traditionally
features prawns (shrimp) and pork.
Another way of eating these pancakes
is to take a lettuce leaf, place
a pancake portion inside it, top it
with herbs and dressing, then wrap
it up and eat it after dipping it in
the dressing.

Tomato salad with mint pepper dressing, raita and poppadoms

800 g (1 lb 12 oz) mixed tomatoes, such
  as black Russian, ox heart, vine-ripened,
  grape and cherry tomatoes
½ small red onion, very thinly sliced
1 green chilli, thinly sliced
1½ tablespoons peanut oil
1 teaspoon black mustard seeds
1 teaspoon freshly ground black pepper
4 garlic cloves, finely chopped
1 tablespoon finely chopped fresh ginger
1 tablespoon lime juice
1 tablespoon vegetable oil, plus extra,
  for pan-frying
2 teaspoons soft brown sugar
1 teaspoon sea salt
1 small handful mint leaves
8 cumin-spiced poppadoms

Raita
1 Lebanese (short) cucumber, chopped
200 g (7 oz) Greek-style yoghurt
1 tablespoon chopped coriander (cilantro)
juice of ½ lemon
½ teaspoon sugar

To make the raita, cut the cucumber into quarters lengthways and remove the seeds. Finely chop the cucumber and place in a small bowl with the remaining raita ingredients. Mix well and season to taste with sea salt and freshly ground black pepper. Set aside.

Cut the tomatoes into slices, halves or quarters, depending on their size. Place in a serving bowl with the onion and chilli.

Heat the peanut oil in a small frying pan over medium heat. Add the mustard seeds, pepper, garlic and ginger and cook for 1 minute, or until the garlic is light golden. Add the lime juice, vegetable oil, sugar and salt. Mix together well, then remove from the heat.

Pour the spice mixture over the tomatoes and gently mix to combine. Scatter with the mint.

Cook the poppadoms following the packet directions.

Serve the tomato salad with the poppadoms and raita.

Preparation time: 45 minutes   **Cooking time:** 55 minutes   **Serves:** 4–6

Lemongrass, corn and coconut soup

1½ tablespoons coarsely chopped
   fresh ginger
2 garlic cloves, chopped
2 lemongrass stems, white part only,
   thinly sliced
½ teaspoon ground turmeric
½ teaspoon chilli flakes, or to taste
60 ml (2 fl oz/¼ cup) peanut oil
1 large brown onion, finely chopped
4 corn cobs, kernels removed
2 desiree or other all-purpose potatoes
   (about 325 g/11½ oz), peeled and cut
   into 5 mm (¼ inch) cubes
1.25 litres (44 fl oz/5 cups) vegetable
   stock
2½ tablespoons soy sauce
400 ml (14 fl oz) tin coconut cream
2 spring onions (scallions), thinly sliced
ground white pepper, to taste
1 small handful chopped coriander
   (cilantro) leaves
2 kaffir lime leaves, very thinly sliced
1 small red chilli, or to taste, thinly sliced
80 g (2¾ oz/½ cup) roasted peanuts,
   coarsely chopped

In a small food processor, combine the ginger, garlic, lemongrass, turmeric and chilli flakes and 1 tablespoon of the oil. Blend until a coarse paste forms.

Heat the remaining oil in a large saucepan over medium–low heat. Add the onion and corn and cook, stirring often, for 10 minutes, or until the corn is starting to soften.

Add the ginger mixture and potato, and stir until well combined. Cook over low heat for 2 minutes, or until aromatic.

Stir in the stock, soy sauce and coconut cream and slowly bring to a simmer. Simmer gently for 35–40 minutes, or until the corn and potato are very tender.

Transfer 750 ml (26 fl oz/3 cups) of the soup to a food processor and blend to a smooth purée. Return the puréed soup to the pan and reheat gently. Stir in the spring onion and season to taste with sea salt and ground white pepper.

Ladle the soup into serving bowls. Serve garnished with the coriander, lime leaves, chilli and peanuts.

If fresh corn isn't available, you could use about 600 g (1 lb 5 oz/4 cups) frozen corn in this recipe.

Thai tofu salad

You can turn this dish into a vegetarian version of the popular Thai appetiser 'larb', which is traditionally an aromatic, spicy mixture of fried ground chicken or pork served in crisp lettuce cups. Instead of using cubed tofu in the salad, crumble it and briefly marinate it in the soy sauce mixture with the shallots, lemongrass, chilli flakes and lime leaves. Toss the herbs, pineapple and tomato through just before serving the mixture in iceberg lettuce cups.

50 g (1¾ oz/¼ cup) white sticky (glutinous) rice
2½ tablespoons finely grated palm sugar (jaggery)
2½ tablespoons lime juice
2 tablespoons soy sauce
1 tablespoon peanut oil
600 g (1 lb 5 oz) firm tofu, drained well and cut into 2 cm (¾ inch) cubes
5–6 red Asian shallots, peeled and thinly sliced, or 1 small red onion, halved and thinly sliced
1 lemongrass stem, white part only, very thinly sliced
1 teaspoon chilli flakes, or to taste
1 handful mint leaves
1 handful coriander (cilantro) leaves
1 handful Thai basil leaves
6 kaffir lime leaves, very thinly sliced
pineapple chunks, to serve
chopped tomatoes, to serve
steamed jasmine rice, to serve

Place the rice in a heavy-based frying pan over medium–low heat. Dry-roast for 8–10 minutes, or until light golden and toasted. Remove from the heat and allow to cool, then transfer to an electric spice grinder or small food processor and grind until a coarse powder forms. Set aside.

In a small bowl, mix together the palm sugar, lime juice and soy sauce, stirring to dissolve the sugar. Set aside.

Heat the oil in a frying pan over high heat. Add the tofu in batches and fry for 3 minutes, or until golden, turning to brown all over.

Return all the tofu to the pan and add the shallot, lemongrass and soy sauce mixture. Cook for 1–2 minutes, or until the mixture starts to bubble. Transfer to a large bowl and add the chilli flakes, herbs and lime leaves. Gently toss to combine.

Divide the salad among serving bowls. Top with some pineapple and tomato as desired. Sprinkle with the toasted rice powder and serve with steamed jasmine rice.

Preparation time: 45 minutes   Cooking time: 20 minutes   Serves: 4

Preparation time: 40 minutes
plus 30 minutes standing

Cooking time: 35 minutes

Serves: 6

Red lentil koftas with tahini garlic sauce

250 g (9 oz/1 cup) red lentils
100 g (3½ oz/½ cup) fine burghul (bulgur)
2 tablespoons olive oil, plus extra, for
  moistening
1 small brown onion, finely chopped
1 garlic clove, crushed
1 teaspoon cayenne pepper
1 teaspoon sweet paprika
2 teaspoons ground cumin
2 tablespoons tomato paste
  (concentrated purée)
3 spring onions (scallions), trimmed
  and very thinly sliced
1 tablespoon lemon juice, or to taste
1 handful flat-leaf (Italian) parsley leaves,
  finely chopped, plus extra, to garnish
small lettuce leaves, to serve
lemon wedges, to serve

Tahini garlic sauce
1 garlic clove, thinly sliced
a pinch of sea salt
125 g (4 oz/½ cup) tahini
1 tablespoon lemon juice
1 tablespoon olive oil

Put the lentils in a saucepan with 500 ml
(17 fl oz/2 cups) water. Bring to the boil over
medium heat, then reduce the heat to a simmer.
Cover and cook, stirring occasionally, for
25 minutes, or until the lentils are soft and
have absorbed all the water. Stir the burghul
through, then cover and remove from the heat.

Meanwhile, to make the tahini garlic sauce,
place the garlic and salt in a mortar and pound
with a pestle until the garlic forms a paste.
(Alternatively you can use a small food processor.)
Add the tahini, lemon juice and olive oil and
process or mix until well combined. Set aside.

Heat the olive oil in a large frying pan over
medium heat. Add the onion and cook for
3–4 minutes, stirring often. Add the garlic and
spices and cook for a further 2 minutes, or until
the onion is browned and the spices are aromatic.
Stir in the tomato paste and season to taste with
sea salt and freshly ground black pepper. Set
aside to cool.

Transfer the onion mixture to a large bowl.
Add the lentil mixture, spring onion, lemon juice
and parsley. Season to taste and mix together
well. If the mixture is dry, add some extra olive oil
a little at a time until the mixture holds its shape.

Roll small amounts of the mixture into
walnut-sized balls and make an indentation in
the top of each using your fingers, or shape into
small cigars about 5 cm (2 inches) long. Place on
a tray, then cover and leave to stand at cool room
temperature for 30 minutes to allow the flavours
to develop.

Serve the koftas at room temperature on a
bed of lettuce, sprinkled with extra parsley and
drizzled with the garlic tahini sauce, with lemon
wedges on the side.

**Popular in the Middle East, tahini
is an oily paste made from ground
sesame seeds. It has a nutty taste
and is sold in supermarkets and
health food stores.**

Thai eggs with sweet and spicy sauce

Also known as sweet soy sauce, kecap manis is a thick, dark, sweet soy sauce used in Indonesian cooking as a seasoning and condiment, particularly with satays.

300 g (10½ oz/1½ cups) jasmine rice
1 tablespoon peanut oil
1 tablespoon finely chopped lemongrass, white part only
1 tablespoon finely grated fresh ginger
700 g (1 lb 9 oz) vine-ripened tomatoes, chopped
1 tablespoon soy sauce
1 tablespoon kecap manis
ground white pepper, to taste
vegetable oil, for deep-frying
4 eggs
3 spring onions (scallions), cut into long shreds
1 small handful coriander (cilantro) leaves
1 long red chilli, thinly sliced

Cook the rice following the packet directions.

Meanwhile, heat the peanut oil in a large frying pan over medium–high heat. Add the lemongrass and ginger and cook, stirring, for 1 minute, or until aromatic. Add the tomato, soy sauce and kecap manis. Cook, stirring occasionally, for 10 minutes, or until the tomato has softened and the sauce has thickened. Season to taste with ground white pepper.

Fill a large wok one-third full of vegetable oil. Heat the oil over medium–high heat to 180°C (350°F), or until a cube of bread dropped into the oil browns in 15 seconds. Break one egg into a cup. Carefully pour the egg into the hot oil and cook, without stirring, for 2–3 minutes. When the egg is almost cooked, carefully remove it from the oil using a slotted spoon — the egg will continue cooking after it has been removed. Drain the egg on paper towels. Repeat with the remaining eggs.

Divide the rice among serving bowls. Top each bowl with the tomato mixture and an egg. Garnish with the spring onion, coriander and chilli, and serve.

Preparation time: 20 minutes   **Cooking time:** 30 minutes   **Serves:** 4

Preparation time: 45 minutes **Cooking time:** 20 minutes **Makes:** 34

Vietnamese rice paper rolls

3 eggs, lightly beaten
1½ tablespoons peanut oil
200 g (7 oz) firm tofu, drained and cut
   into 5 mm (¼ inch)-thick slices
2 red Asian shallots, finely diced
2 tablespoons soy sauce
500 g (1 lb 2 oz) jicama, peeled and
   grated, and excess liquid squeezed out
2 carrots, coarsely grated
100 g (3½ oz) bean sprouts, tails trimmed
60 ml (2 fl oz/¼ cup) hoisin sauce, plus
   extra, to serve
2 teaspoons chilli sauce
4 spring onions (scallions), cut into thin
   strips about 4 cm (1½ inches) long
1 bunch Vietnamese mint, leaves picked
50 g (1¾ oz/⅓ cup) roasted peanuts,
   chopped, plus extra, to serve
34 rice paper wrappers, about 22 cm
   (8½ inches) in diameter

Whisk the eggs in a small bowl, then season with sea salt and freshly ground black pepper.

Heat 1 teaspoon of the oil in a small non-stick frying pan over medium heat. Add half the egg mixture, swirling to create a thin omelette. Cook for 2 minutes, or until the egg has just set, then transfer to a plate. Repeat with the remaining egg, adding a little more oil to the pan as needed. Allow the omelettes to cool, then roll them up and cut them crossways, to form thin strips. Set aside.

Heat another 2 teaspoons of the oil in a larger non-stick frying pan over high heat. Add the tofu slices and cook for 2 minutes on each side, or until lightly browned. Remove from the pan and allow to cool, then cut into thin strips. Set aside.

Wipe the pan clean and heat the remaining oil over medium heat. Add the shallot and cook, stirring, for 2 minutes. Add the soy sauce, jicama and carrot, and cook, uncovered, for 6–8 minutes, or until the vegetables are tender, stirring often. Transfer to a bowl and allow to cool. Season to taste, add the bean sprouts and stir to combine.

Combine the hoisin and chilli sauce in a small bowl. Place the sauce, egg strips, tofu, jicama mixture, spring onion, mint and peanuts in neat piles on a clean work surface.

Place one rice paper round in a bowl of lukewarm water for 10 seconds, or until soft and pliable. Remove from the water and place on a clean tea towel (dish towel). Spread a small amount of the hoisin mixture in the centre of the round, then add a small amount of the omelette, tofu, 1 tablespoon of the jicama mixture, a strip of spring onion, one mint leaf and a sprinkle of peanuts. Fold in each side of the rice paper, then roll up firmly to enclose the filling. Repeat with the remaining rice paper wrappers and filling.

Serve immediately with the extra hoisin sauce sprinkled with the extra peanuts.

Hailing from South America and Mexico, and similar in appearance to a tan-coloured turnip or large radish, jicama is a sweet, edible root from the legume family. It has a thin, papery skin which should be peeled before eating; its inner white flesh has a crisp, starchy texture like that of a raw potato. Raw jicama tastes quite similar to an apple or pear. It is available from good greengrocers, some Asian grocery stores and larger supermarkets.

Hoisin sauce is a thick red-brown sauce made from soya beans, garlic, sugar and spices. It has a distinctive salty-sweet-spicy flavour and is used in cooking and as a dipping sauce.

Barley, celery and yoghurt soup

Pearl barley is especially wonderful in winter soups. As the soup cooks, the barley starch helps thicken it while providing flavour, texture and creaminess. Pearl barley is also a good alternative to rice in a risotto. You'll find it in supermarkets and health food stores.

225 g (8 oz/1 cup) pearl barley
25 g (1 oz) butter
2 brown onions, finely chopped
2 garlic cloves, crushed
½ head of celery, trimmed and finely chopped
1.5 litres (52 fl oz/6 cups) vegetable stock
1 tablespoon dried mint
3 egg yolks, lightly beaten
60 ml (2 fl oz/¼ cup) lemon juice
1½ teaspoons finely grated lemon rind
625 g (1 lb 6 oz/2½ cups) Greek-style yoghurt
35 g (1¼ oz/¼ cup) plain (all-purpose) flour
shredded mint, to garnish
Turkish bread, to serve

Bring a saucepan of water to the boil. Add the barley and cook for 35–40 minutes, or until tender. Drain well and set aside.

Meanwhile, heat the butter in a large saucepan over medium heat. Add the onion and garlic and cook, stirring, for 5 minutes, or until the onion is starting to soften. Stir in the celery, then cover the pan and cook, stirring often, for 8 minutes, or until the celery is starting to soften. Add the stock and dried mint and bring back to a simmer. Cook for 10 minutes, or until the celery is very tender.

In a bowl, whisk together the egg yolks, lemon juice, lemon rind and yoghurt. Add the flour and whisk until smooth.

Add 500 ml (17 fl oz/2 cups) of the hot soup mixture to the yoghurt mixture and mix until smooth. Pour the mixture back into the soup. Add the cooked barley and stir over medium heat until the mixture comes back to a simmer. Cook, stirring, for a further 4–5 minutes, or until the soup thickens slightly. Season to taste with sea salt and freshly ground black pepper.

Ladle the soup into serving bowls and garnish with the mint. Serve with Turkish bread.

Preparation time: 30 minutes   **Cooking time:** 45 minutes   **Serves:** 6

Preparation time: 15 minutes
plus 30 minutes standing

Cooking time: Nil

Serves: 4

Radicchio salad with fennel, grapefruit, blue cheese and almonds

½ red onion, thinly sliced
1 pink grapefruit
1 head of radicchio, trimmed, washed and drained
1 fennel bulb, trimmed, tough core removed, then cut in half lengthways and thinly sliced
50 g (1¾ oz/⅓ cup) smoked almonds, coarsely chopped
50 g (1¾ oz) Danish blue cheese, crumbled

Garlic mustard dressing
1 egg yolk
1 garlic clove, crushed
1 tablespoon sherry vinegar
1 tablespoon dijon mustard
100 ml (3½ fl oz) light olive oil

Put the onion in a small bowl, cover with cold water and leave to stand for 30 minutes. Drain well and set aside.

Remove the skin and pith from the grapefruit using a sharp serrated knife. Holding the grapefruit over a bowl to catch any juices, remove each segment by cutting close to the membrane to release the whole segment. Reserve the juice and place the segments in a large salad bowl.

Slice or tear the radicchio into the salad bowl. Add the fennel and drained onion and gently toss to combine.

To make the garlic mustard dressing, whisk the egg yolk, garlic, vinegar and mustard in a large bowl until well combined. Whisking constantly, add 60 ml (2 fl oz/¼ cup) of the olive oil, a teaspoon at a time. Very slowly add the remaining oil in a thin steady stream until the mixture is thickened and emulsified. Whisk in the reserved grapefruit juice and a little warm water to thin the dressing, if necessary — the dressing should have a creamy, coating consistency. Season to taste with sea salt and freshly ground black pepper.

Drizzle the dressing over the salad and toss to coat. Scatter with the almonds and cheese, and serve.

If you're not fond of blue cheese, you can substitute soft feta or goat's cheese in this salad.

Indonesian spring rolls

500 ml (17 fl oz/2 cups) peanut oil
4 spring onions (scallions),
  finely chopped
1 garlic clove, chopped
2 small shiitake mushrooms, finely
  chopped
100 g (3½ oz) enoki mushrooms,
  trimmed, separated and cut into
  8 cm (3 inch) lengths
1 small carrot, cut into fine matchsticks
90 g (3¼ oz/1 cup) bean sprouts,
  tails trimmed
75 g (2½ oz/½ cup) finely shredded
  jicama (see note page 77)
2 tablespoons toasted peanuts, chopped
4 tablespoons coriander (cilantro) leaves,
  coarsely chopped
1 tablespoon kecap manis, plus extra,
  to serve
¼ teaspoon sesame oil
10 frozen 12.5 cm (4½ inch) spring roll
  wrappers, thawed
1 egg white, beaten

To make the filling, heat 1 tablespoon of the peanut oil in a non-stick frying pan over medium heat. Add the spring onion and garlic and cook, stirring, for 1 minute. Add the mushrooms, carrot, bean sprouts and jicama and cook for a further 2 minutes, or until softened. Transfer the mixture to a bowl.

Add the peanuts, coriander, kecap manis and sesame oil to the mushroom mixture. Toss until well combined, then season to taste with sea salt and freshly ground black pepper.

Place one spring roll wrapper on a clean work surface. Brush the edges lightly with egg white. Place 1 heaped tablespoon of the filling along one edge of the wrapper. Take the bottom edge and enclose the filling, then tuck in the two side edges. Brush again with egg white and roll up firmly. Place the spring roll on a plate, seam side down. Repeat with the remaining filling and wrappers.

Heat the remaining peanut oil in a small saucepan over medium–high heat to 180ºC (350ºF), or until a cube of bread dropped into the oil browns in 15 seconds. Working in batches, deep-fry the spring rolls for 2–3 minutes, or until golden and crisp. Drain on paper towels.

Serve hot, with extra kecap manis for dipping.

✳ **Preparation time:** 35 minutes ✳ **Cooking time:** 20 minutes ✳ **Makes:** 10

Chinese hot and sour soup

4 dried wood ear mushrooms
  (about 20 g/¾ oz)
6 dried shiitake mushrooms (about
  30 g/1 oz)
2 tablespoons Chinese black vinegar
2 tablespoons rice vinegar
2 tablespoons soy sauce
1 tablespoon light soy sauce
1½ tablespoons sugar
1 teaspoon sea salt
2 litres (70 fl oz/8 cups) vegetable stock
125 g (4½ oz/½ cup) tinned sliced
  bamboo shoots, rinsed and cut into
  thin shreds
200 g (7 oz) silken tofu, drained and cut
  into 1 cm (½ inch) cubes

Put the mushrooms in a heatproof bowl and pour in 600 ml (21 fl oz) boiling water. Leave to soak for 30 minutes.

Drain the mushrooms well, reserving the soaking liquid. Strain the liquid through a sieve lined with muslin (cheesecloth). Reserve 250 ml (9 fl oz/1 cup) of the soaking liquid and discard the rest. Trim the stalks from the mushrooms and cut the larger mushrooms into three.

Combine the Chinese black vinegar, rice vinegar, soy sauces, sugar and salt in a small bowl. Stir to dissolve the sugar.

Pour the vegetable stock and reserved mushroom liquid into a saucepan. Bring to the boil, then reduce the heat to a simmer. Stir in the soy and vinegar mixture and simmer for a further 20 minutes.

Add the mushrooms and bamboo shoots to the soup and simmer for a final 5–6 minutes.

Ladle the soup into serving bowls and serve topped with the tofu.

Wood ear mushrooms are actually a black tree fungus, also known as 'cloud ear' fungus. They have little flavour of their own, but are valued for their crunchy texture. Asian grocery stores most commonly sell them in their dried form. The dried fungus should be reconstituted in warm water for 15–30 minutes, or until it swells to about five times its original size. Chinese black vinegar is made from rice and is sharper than white rice vinegars. It is traditionally used in stir-fries, soups and dipping sauces, and is also available from Asian grocery stores. The best black vinegars come from the Chinese province of Zhejiang.

Mushroom salad with ciabatta croutons and mint salsa verde

❋

Sherry vinegar is sometimes called sherry wine vinegar or Jerez vinegar. Made from sherry, its deep, complex flavour enhances sauces, soups and dressings. The finest sherry vinegar is produced in Spain's 'sherry triangle' in the province of Cádiz, and is aged in American oak for at least six months. You'll find it in speciality food stores.

12 medium mushroom flats
2 garlic cloves, crushed
80 ml (2½ fl oz/⅓ cup) olive oil
100 g (3½ oz) ciabatta bread, torn into
 1 cm (½ inch) chunks
150 g (5½ oz) rocket (arugula), trimmed
 and coarsely chopped
50 g (1¾ oz/½ cup) shaved
 parmesan cheese
2 tablespoons lemon juice

Mint salsa verde
1 French shallot, finely chopped
2 teaspoons sherry vinegar
60 ml (2 fl oz/¼ cup) extra virgin olive oil
1 tablespoon chopped mint leaves
2½ tablespoons chopped flat-leaf
 (Italian) parsley

Preheat the oven to 180°C (350°F/Gas 4).

Combine the mint salsa verde ingredients in a bowl. Mix together and set aside.

Place the mushrooms in a single layer in a roasting tin. Combine the garlic with half the olive oil, then drizzle over the mushrooms. Season to taste with sea salt and freshly ground black pepper.

Place the bread on a baking tray in a single layer and drizzle with the remaining oil.

Bake the bread and the mushrooms for 20 minutes, or until the mushrooms are tender. Remove the mushrooms from the oven and set aside.

Bake the bread for a further 10 minutes, or until golden and crisp. Remove from the oven.

Place the rocket, parmesan, lemon juice and ciabatta croutons in a bowl. Add the salsa verde and mix well.

Arrange the mushrooms in shallow serving bowls. Pile the rocket mixture over the top and serve.

Preparation time: 15 minutes   **Cooking time:** 15 minutes   **Serves:** 4

Warm jerusalem artichoke and potato purée with hazelnut dukkah

2 large pitta breads
olive oil, for brushing and drizzling
1 desiree or other all-purpose potato
  (about 200 g/7 oz), peeled and chopped
150 g (5½ oz) jerusalem artichokes,
  peeled and chopped
1 garlic clove, crushed
35 g (1¼ oz/¼ cup) finely grated
  gruyère cheese
80 ml (2½ fl oz/⅓ cup) milk

Hazelnut dukkah
2 tablespoons chopped roasted hazelnuts
1 teaspoon cumin seeds
2 tablespoons chopped flat-leaf
  (Italian) parsley

Preheat the oven to 180°C (350°F/Gas 4). Brush the pitta breads with olive oil and tear into bite-sized pieces. Place on a baking tray in a single layer and bake for 8–10 minutes, or until golden and crisp.

Meanwhile, bring a small saucepan of salted water to the boil. Add the potato and artichoke and cook for 10 minutes, or until very tender. Drain well, then purée the mixture by pushing it through a potato ricer or sieve (don't use a food processor or the mixture will become gluey). Allow to cool slightly, then stir in the garlic, gruyère and milk. Season to taste with sea salt and freshly ground black pepper. Keep warm.

To make the hazelnut dukkah, place the hazelnuts in a food processor and blend until finely chopped; tip into a small serving bowl. Heat a small non-stick frying pan over low heat, then add the cumin seeds and dry-roast for 1 minute, or until aromatic, shaking the pan often so they don't burn. Lightly crush the cumin seeds in a mortar using a pestle, then add to the hazelnuts. Stir in the parsley and season to taste with sea salt and freshly ground black pepper.

Transfer the warm artichoke and potato purée to a serving bowl. Drizzle with olive oil and sprinkle with freshly ground black pepper. Serve with the pitta crisps and hazelnut dukkah.

No relation to the globe artichoke, jerusalem artichokes are small tubers from the sunflower family. Their sweet, earthy flavour makes them ideal for soups and purées. As you peel them, drop them into a bowl of water with a splash of lemon juice to stop them discolouring.

Stuffed vine leaves with egg and lemon sauce

Vine leaves are the young, large green leaves of the grape vine, used in Greece and the Middle East to wrap foods for cooking. They are sold in tins, jars, packets or in brine in Mediterranean and Middle Eastern grocery stores. Vine leaves in brine should be rinsed before using to remove excess saltiness. Before using fresh vine leaves, simmer them in water for 10 minutes to soften them.

100 g (3½ oz/½ cup) long-grain white rice
400 g (14 oz) tin chickpeas, rinsed and drained well
1 ripe tomato, peeled and chopped
1 brown onion, finely chopped
2 garlic cloves, finely chopped
¼ cup chopped flat-leaf (Italian) parsley
1½ tablespoons chopped dill
1 teaspoon ground cinnamon
2 tablespoons tomato paste (concentrated purée)
225 g (8 oz) vine leaves in brine, rinsed and dried
2 tablespoons lemon juice

Egg and lemon sauce
375 ml (13 fl oz/1½ cups) vegetable stock
80 ml (2½ fl oz/⅓ cup) lemon juice, plus extra, to taste
2 teaspoons finely grated lemon rind
6 large egg yolks

Place the rice in a bowl, pour enough boiling water over to cover, then leave to soak for 30 minutes. Drain well.

Mash the chickpeas in a bowl using a fork. Add the rice, tomato, onion, garlic, herbs, cinnamon and tomato paste and mix until well combined.

Use about five vine leaves to line the base of a large saucepan (this will prevent the stuffed vine leaves from sticking to the pan). Lay another vine leaf on a clean work surface and place 1 tablespoon of the rice mixture across the centre, near the stem end. Fold the sides of the vine leaf over the filling, then roll the vine leaf into a cigar shape. Repeat with the remaining vine leaves and filling.

Place the stuffed leaves in the lined saucepan, packing them in tight layers. Add the lemon juice and about 350 ml (12 fl oz) water, or enough to cover the leaves. Place a small plate directly over the stuffed leaves to keep them immersed in the liquid, then cover the saucepan with a lid. Bring the liquid to a simmer, then cook over low heat for 1 hour, adding a little extra water as necessary to stop the leaves cooking dry.

Meanwhile, make the egg and lemon sauce. Heat the stock, lemon juice and lemon rind in a small saucepan until just boiling; remove from the heat. Lightly beat the egg yolks in a bowl, then pour some of the hot liquid over them and stir until well combined. Pour the egg mixture into the hot stock mixture and cook over medium–low heat, stirring constantly with a wooden spoon, for 15–20 minutes, or until the sauce has thickened slightly (do not simmer). Taste and stir in extra lemon juice if needed.

Serve the vine leaves warm, with the warm egg and lemon sauce.

Preparation time: 35 minutes
plus 30 minutes soaking

Cooking time: 1 hour

Makes:
about 20

Preparation time: 15 minutes   **Cooking time:** 35 minutes   **Serves:** 6

Stuffed tomatoes with baked yoghurt

12 large, firm vine-ripened or organic
  tomatoes (about 1.8 kg/4 lb),
  with stems on
olive oil, for drizzling

Couscous stuffing
125 g (4½ oz/⅔ cup) instant couscous
125 ml (4 fl oz/½ cup) vegetable stock
4 garlic cloves, finely chopped
1 tablespoon olive oil
100 g (3½ oz/⅔ cup) crumbled
  feta cheese
75 g (2½ oz) pitted green olives, chopped
400 g (14 oz) tin chickpeas, rinsed
  and drained
¼ cup chopped mint leaves
¼ cup chopped flat-leaf (Italian) parsley

Baked yoghurt
500 g (1 lb 2 oz/2 cups) Greek-style
  yoghurt
1 garlic clove, crushed
1 teaspoon oregano
2 eggs, plus 2 egg yolks
65 g (2½ oz/½ cup) crumbled feta cheese
2 tablespoons finely chopped flat-leaf
  (Italian) parsley

Preheat the oven to 180°C (350°F/Gas 4).

Using a serrated knife, carefully cut off the top of each tomato in one piece to make a lid about 1 cm (½ inch) thick. Using a teaspoon, gently remove the seeds from inside the tomato and the tomato top, and scoop out the flesh, leaving a firm shell. Reserve the seeds and any juice for another use; dice the scooped-out tomato flesh and reserve.

To make the couscous stuffing, place the couscous in a large heatproof bowl and bring the stock to the boil in a small saucepan. Pour the hot stock over the couscous, then cover and leave to stand for 3 minutes. Fluff the couscous with a fork.

Add the reserved tomato flesh and the remaining stuffing ingredients and mix well. Season to taste with sea salt and freshly ground black pepper.

Spoon the couscous stuffing into each tomato and replace the lids. Place the tomatoes in a baking dish and drizzle with olive oil; set aside.

For the baked yoghurt, place the yoghurt, garlic and oregano in a small saucepan over low heat and gently stir until hot — do not allow to boil. Remove from the heat and keep warm.

In a small bowl, lightly beat the eggs and egg yolks and season to taste. Slowly pour the heated yoghurt into the eggs, whisking continuously until combined. Stir in the feta and parsley.

Pour the mixture into six 125 ml (4 fl oz/ ½ cup) ramekins. Place the ramekins in a deep baking dish and pour enough boiling water into the baking dish to come halfway up the side of the ramekins.

Transfer the yoghurt and tomato baking dishes to the oven, keeping them both uncovered. Bake the yoghurt for 30 minutes, or until set; remove the ramekins from the baking dish and stand for 5 minutes. Bake the tomatoes for a further 5 minutes, or until the filling is heated through.

Serve the tomatoes with the baked yoghurt.

Fritto misto with tarragon mayonnaise

In Italian 'fritto misto' simply means 'mixed fried' and refers to an assemblage of ingredients that are quickly deep-fried in a batter. Experiment with your own combinations of ingredients.

225 g (8 oz/1½ cups) self-raising flour
300 g (10½ oz/1½ cups) coarse semolina
600 ml (21 fl oz) buttermilk
16 large sage leaves
1 tablespoon black olive paste
1 litre (35 fl oz/4 cups) vegetable oil,
  for deep-frying
12 stuffed green olives
3 sebago or other floury potatoes (about
  600 g/1 lb 5 oz), peeled and cut into
  5 mm (¼ inch)-thick slices
8 baby carrots, trimmed, peeled and
  cut in half lengthways
12 asparagus spears, trimmed
sea salt, to sprinkle
lemon cheeks, to serve

Tarragon mayonnaise
250 g (9 fl oz/1 cup) good-quality
  whole-egg mayonnaise
2 tablespoons finely chopped tarragon
2 teaspoons lemon juice

In a small serving bowl, combine the tarragon mayonnaise ingredients. Cover and refrigerate until serving time.

Combine the flour and semolina in a bowl, then pour the buttermilk into a separate bowl. Set aside.

Sandwich two sage leaves together with ½ teaspoon of the black olive paste. Repeat with the remaining sage and olive paste. Set aside.

Heat the oil in a deep-fryer or saucepan to 180°C (350°F), or until a cube of bread dropped into the oil browns in 15 seconds.

Dip each ingredient separately into the buttermilk, then into the flour mixture, and then place them on a tray. The olives, potatoes, carrots and asparagus should be coated a second time after letting the first coat set for 2 minutes.

Working with five or so pieces at a time so the oil temperature doesn't drop too much, fry each batch for 2–3 minutes, or until golden all over, turning regularly. Remove each batch using a large slotted spoon, gently tapping the spoon on the edge of the saucepan to remove the excess oil. Drain well on paper towels and repeat with the remaining battered vegetables.

Serve the fritto misto immediately sprinkled with sea salt, with the tarragon mayonnaise and lemon cheeks on the side.

Preparation time: 25 minutes   **Cooking time:** 20 minutes   **Serves:** 4

Mains

Stuffed zucchini with minted yoghurt and cumin-spiced tomato sauce • Blue cheese mille-feuille with glazed red onion and fig and cress salad • Chickpea, corn and semi-dried tomato patties with rocket salad • Bean, asparagus and potato salad with smoked paprika romesco • Pizza with pear, radicchio and walnuts • Mexican bean casserole on cornbread with avocado salsa • Eggplant curry • Baked wholemeal crepes with asparagus and leek and basil cream • Persian vegetable and fruit stew • White bean and silverbeet timbales with roast tomato sauce • Green vegetable curry • Clay pot mushrooms, tofu and vermicelli • Greek red lentil and potato rissoles • Green vegetable bake with pine nut and pecorino crumble • Mushroom and spinach lasagne • Kung pao with broccoli and peanuts • Fettuccine with roast fennel, saffron, olives and breadcrumbs • Dry potato curry with egg and peas • Puy lentils with chestnuts and spinach on soft polenta • Linguine with green beans, potato, and mint and almond pesto • Polenta and provolone soufflés with red wine–rosemary capsicum • Cauliflower and white bean korma • Roasted pumpkin gnocchi with three-cheese sauce • Tofu burgers with sweet chilli mayonnaise • Baked turlu turlu with haloumi • Pad see hew • Caramelised onion tarte tatin • Spiced sweet potato coils with couscous salad • Vegetable skewers with parsnip skordalia • Carrot and almond gougère • Five-spice braised eggplant with tofu and bok choy • Silverbeet, rice and parmesan tart • Mee rebus • Salt and pepper tofu with snow peas • Vegetarian 'meatballs' in North African-spiced tomato sauce • Tofu steak with fried eggplant, daikon and red miso dressing • Mushroom, dill and cream cheese coulibiac • Spicy chickpea pot pie • Georgian bean pie • Thai pineapple and tofu fried rice • Tunisian vegetable stew with lemon pickle • Beetroot, red wine and borlotti bean risotto • Baked ricotta-stuffed eggplant rolls • Broad bean and pea rotolo • Chillies rellenos

Preparation time: 30 minutes   **Cooking time:** 1 hour 20 minutes   **Serves:** 4

Stuffed zucchini with minted yoghurt and cumin-spiced tomato sauce

12 Lebanese zucchini (courgettes),
   measuring 12–15 cm (4½–6 inches)
   in length
150 g (5½ oz/¾ cup) long-grain white rice
2 tablespoons olive oil
1 large brown onion, finely chopped
1 tablespoon pine nuts
¼ cup finely chopped flat-leaf (Italian)
   parsley, plus extra, to garnish
¼ cup finely chopped mint leaves, plus
   extra, to garnish
½ teaspoon ground cinnamon
½ teaspoon ground allspice
200 g (7 oz/1⅓ cups) feta cheese,
   crumbled
halved cherry tomatoes, to serve

Cumin-spiced tomato sauce
1 tablespoon olive oil
1 brown onion, finely chopped
2 garlic cloves, crushed
60 g (2¼ oz/¼ cup) tomato paste
   (concentrated purée)
2½ teaspoons ground cumin
1 dried bay leaf
400 g (14 oz) tin chopped tomatoes
375 ml (13 fl oz/1½ cups) vegetable stock

Minted yoghurt
250 g (9 oz/1 cup) Greek-style yoghurt
1 garlic clove, crushed with a little sea salt
1 tablespoon chopped mint leaves

To make the cumin-spiced tomato sauce, heat the olive oil in a saucepan over medium heat. Cook the onion, stirring, for 5–8 minutes, or until softened. Stir in the garlic, tomato paste and cumin and cook, stirring, for 2 minutes. Add the remaining ingredients and stir to combine well. Bring to the boil, remove from the heat and set aside.

Combine the minted yoghurt ingredients in a small bowl. Mix well, then cover and refrigerate until required.

Preheat the oven to 180°C (350°F/Gas 4). Trim about 1 cm (½ inch) from each end of the zucchini. Using an apple corer or a narrow sharp knife and a teaspoon, carefully cut out the flesh from the centre of each zucchini, leaving at least a 5 mm (¼ inch)-thick shell all around. Reserve the removed flesh.

Wash the rice until the water runs clear, then drain well and set aside. Heat the olive oil in a frying pan over medium heat. Cook the onion, stirring, for 5–8 minutes, or until softened. Add the pine nuts and cook for a further 2 minutes, stirring occasionally. Tip the mixture into a bowl, then stir in the rice, herbs, spices and feta until well combined. Season to taste with sea salt and freshly ground black pepper.

Fill the hollowed-out zucchini with the rice stuffing until three-quarters filled. Use the reserved flesh as a cork to plug the ends of each zucchini. Spoon one-third of the tomato sauce over the base of a baking dish just large enough to hold the zucchini snugly. Place the zucchini side by side over the sauce, then pour the remaining sauce over the top. Seal the baking dish with foil. Bake for 1 hour, or until the rice and zucchini are tender.

Serve the zucchini warm or hot, drizzled with the sauce, topped with the cherry tomato halves and garnished with the parsley and mint. Accompany with the minted yoghurt.

Lebanese zucchini are often used in Middle Eastern cooking. They are a speckled pale green colour and have a naturally fuller shape at their base compared to their dark green cousins, which makes them ideal for stuffing. A special corer, called a manakra, is used to remove the zucchini pulp. You can find these in Middle Eastern grocery stores.

Blue cheese mille-feuille with glazed red onion and fig and cress salad

Originally a sweet French creation consisting of thin layers of puff pastry separated by layers of cream or jam with a top covered in icing (confectioners') sugar or icing (frosting), a mille-feuille is now often made as a savoury dish, usually served as a starter. Here it is served as a light main course.

5 small red onions, peeled and sliced into 1 cm (½ inch) rounds
1 teaspoon balsamic vinegar
2 tablespoons olive oil
2 teaspoons brown sugar
80 ml (2½ fl oz/⅓ cup) red wine
2 sheets frozen puff pastry, thawed
20 g (¾ oz) butter, melted
75 g (2½ oz) blue cheese, at room temperature, chopped
125 g (4½ oz) mascarpone cheese, at room temperature
2 tablespoons thickened cream

Fig and cress salad
4 fresh figs, each cut into 4 slices
1 bunch (500 g/1 lb 2 oz) watercress, sprigs picked
1 egg yolk
2 teaspoons dijon mustard
1½ tablespoons red wine vinegar
60 ml (2 fl oz/¼ cup) extra virgin olive oil

Preheat the oven to 200°C (400°F/Gas 6). Line a baking tray with baking paper. Spread the onion on the baking tray, then drizzle with the vinegar and olive oil. Sprinkle with the sugar and season to taste with sea salt and freshly ground black pepper. Bake for 15 minutes, then pour the wine over. Bake for a further 15–20 minutes, or until the onion is golden and tender. Remove from the oven and set aside.

Increase the oven temperature to 220°C (425°F/Gas 7). Line two baking trays with baking paper. Cut each puff pastry sheet into six rectangles, measuring about 12 x 8 cm (4½ x 3¼ inches). Place eight pastry rectangles on one baking tray, prick them all over with a fork, then brush with melted butter. Place a sheet of baking paper over the top, then cover with a baking tray to weigh them down. Bake for 8–10 minutes, or until crisp. Remove from the oven and set aside.

Place the remaining four pastry rectangles on the other lined baking tray; these will be the mille-feuille lids. Prick them all over with a fork, then brush with melted butter. Place a sheet of baking paper over the top, then cover with another baking tray and bake for 5 minutes. Remove the tray and paper and bake for a further 5 minutes, or until golden. Set aside to cool.

In a bowl, whisk the blue cheese, mascarpone and cream until just combined and smooth.

Place four cooled pastry bases on serving plates. Top with half the roasted onion and a spoonful of the blue cheese mixture. Top with another four pastry rectangles, then the rest of the onion and blue cheese. Cover with lids.

To make the fig and cress salad, place the figs and watercress in a serving bowl. In a large bowl, whisk together the egg, mustard and vinegar, then gradually add the olive oil in a thin steady stream, whisking constantly. If necessary, whisk in 1 tablespoon warm water to thin the dressing and season to taste. Pour over the salad and toss gently. Serve with the mille-feuille.

Preparation time: 35 minutes   **Cooking time:** 55 minutes   **Serves:** 4

Preparation time: 20 minutes plus overnight soaking and 30 minutes chilling

Cooking time: 20 minutes

Serves: 4 (makes 8)

Chickpea, corn and semi-dried tomato patties with rocket salad

225 g (8 oz/1 cup) dried chickpeas
1 small brown onion, coarsely chopped
2 garlic cloves
1 tablespoon sweet paprika
1 small red chilli, seeded and chopped
½ teaspoon salt
½ teaspoon freshly ground black pepper
1 egg, lightly whisked
1 handful basil leaves
1 large handful flat-leaf (Italian) parsley
100 g (3½ oz/½ cup) fresh corn kernels, or 100 g (3½ oz/⅔ cup) frozen corn kernels, thawed
30 g (1 oz/¼ cup) chopped semi-dried (sun-blushed) tomatoes
vegetable oil, for deep-frying

Rocket salad
2 large handfuls rocket (arugula) leaves
200 g (7 oz) cherry tomatoes, halved
100 g (3½ oz/1 cup) shaved pecorino cheese
60 ml (2 fl oz/¼ cup) extra virgin olive oil
1 tablespoon lemon juice

Place the chickpeas in a large bowl and cover with cold water. Leave to soak overnight.

Drain the chickpeas and place in a food processor with the onion, garlic, paprika, chilli, salt and pepper. Blend until the chickpeas are the size of coarse breadcrumbs and the consistency is pasty. Add the egg, herbs, half the corn and half the tomato, and blend until the mixture just starts to come together. Transfer the mixture to a bowl. Add the remaining tomato and corn to the mixture. Mix together well, then cover and refrigerate for 30 minutes.

Shape the mixture into 8 patties, about 7 cm (2¾ inches) in diameter.

Preheat the oven to 150°C (300°F/Gas 2). Heat 1 cm (½ inch) oil in a large frying pan over medium heat. Working in batches, cook the patties for 2 minutes on each side, or until a deep golden brown. Drain on paper towels and keep warm in the oven while cooking the remaining patties.

To make the rocket salad, put the rocket, tomatoes and pecorino in a serving bowl. Whisk together the olive oil and lemon juice, and season with sea salt and freshly ground black pepper. Pour the dressing over the salad and toss gently to coat.

Pile the rocket salad on serving plates, top with the patties and serve.

The patties can be prepared a day ahead and stored in an airtight container, in layers separated by baking paper, in the refrigerator until you are ready to cook them.
If using fresh corn, you'll need about 2 cobs.

Bean, asparagus and potato salad with smoked paprika romesco

If you don't have a gas stovetop, you can grill (broil) the capsicums for the romesco sauce. Cut the capsicums into quarters and remove the seeds and membranes. Preheat the grill (broiler) on high. Place the capsicum quarters on a baking tray, skin side up. Grill for 10–15 minutes, or until the skins are blistered and blackened. Transfer to a sealed plastic bag or place in a bowl and cover with plastic wrap or a plate. Allow to cool, then peel off the skin and use as directed. Fresh borlotti beans can be used in place of the tinned beans. They come in long pinkish-red pods splashed with beige. The shelled beans are pale with purplish-pink streaks and have a nutty flavour and creamy texture. You will need about 600 g (1 lb 5 oz) whole pods. Cook the shelled beans by boiling in salted water for 4–5 minutes or until tender.

600 g (1 lb 5 oz) kipfler (fingerling) or
   other waxy potatoes, scrubbed
250 g (9 oz) baby green beans, trimmed
250 g (9 oz) sugar snap peas, trimmed
2 bunches (350 g/12 oz) asparagus
   (about 18 spears), trimmed
400 g (14 oz) tin borlotti (cranberry) beans,
   rinsed and drained
80 g (2¾ oz/⅔ cup) pitted green olives
2 large handfuls rocket (arugula) leaves
2½ tablespoons sherry vinegar
80 ml (2½ fl oz/⅓ cup) extra virgin olive oil
crusty bread, to serve

Smoked paprika romesco

2 large red capsicums (peppers)
50 g (1¾ oz) day-old rustic white bread,
   crusts removed
125 g (4½ oz/¾ cup) blanched almonds
3 garlic cloves, chopped
125 ml (4 fl oz/½ cup) undrained tinned
   chopped tomatoes
1 teaspoon smoked paprika
1 tablespoon sherry vinegar
2½ tablespoons extra virgin olive oil

To make the smoked paprika romesco, place the whole capsicums directly over medium–low gas flames and cook, turning often, for 8–10 minutes, or until charred all over. Remove to a bowl, cover and cool. Quarter the capsicums, then using your hands, remove the seeds and blackened skin — avoid running the capsicums under water or you will lose flavour. Place the capsicums in a food processor with the remaining romesco ingredients and process until a coarse purée forms. Season to taste with sea salt and freshly ground black pepper. Transfer to a serving bowl, cover and set aside.

Meanwhile, bring a saucepan of salted water to the boil. Add the whole potatoes and cook for 10–15 minutes, or until tender. Remove using a slotted spoon, reserving the saucepan of water. Drain the potatoes well and leave to cool.

Add the green beans to the boiling water and cook for 2–3 minutes, or until all the beans are tender. Using a slotted spoon, remove the beans to a colander and drain well, reserving the cooking water.

Add the sugar snap peas to the boiling water and cook for 2 minutes, or until tender, then remove using a slotted spoon and drain well. Finally add the asparagus to the boiling water and cook for 2–3 minutes, or until tender. Drain well.

Cut the potatoes into 1 cm (½ inch)-thick slices, then combine in a large bowl with the blanched vegetables, borlotti beans, olives and rocket. Add the vinegar and olive oil and toss gently to combine.

Place the salad on a serving platter. Spoon some romesco sauce over the top. Serve with the romesco sauce passed separately, with crusty bread on the side.

Preparation time: 40 minutes   **Cooking time:** 35 minutes   **Serves:** 6

Preparation time: 35 minutes
plus 1 hour proving

Cooking time: 25 minutes

Serves: 4

Pizza with pear, radicchio and walnuts

1 head of radicchio, trimmed, washed, patted dry and cut into quarters
60 ml (2 fl oz/¼ cup) olive oil
1 tablespoon honey
3 garlic cloves, crushed
1 teaspoon rosemary, chopped
1 large pear, halved, cored and thinly sliced
100 g (3½ oz/1 cup) walnut halves, chopped
50 g (1¾ oz/½ cup) shaved parmesan cheese
1 tablespoon ready-made balsamic glaze (see note)
rocket (arugula) or extra radicchio leaves, to serve

Pizza dough

260 g (9¼ oz/1¾ cups) plain (all-purpose) flour, plus extra, for dusting
2 teaspoons dried yeast
1 teaspoon sea salt
1 teaspoon caster (superfine) sugar
2 tablespoons extra virgin olive oil, plus extra, for greasing

To make the pizza dough, combine the flour, yeast, salt and sugar in a large bowl. Make a well in the centre. Combine the olive oil with 185 ml (6 fl oz/¾ cup) lukewarm water. Add to the flour mixture and mix until a dough forms. Turn out onto a lightly floured surface and knead for 5 minutes, or until smooth and elastic, adding a little extra flour if the mixture is very sticky. Place in an oiled bowl, turning to coat in the oil, then cover with plastic wrap and stand in a warm, draught-free place for 1 hour, or until doubled in size.

Preheat the oven to 220°C (425°F/Gas 7). Lightly oil two 26 cm (10½ inch) pizza trays and dust with a little extra flour. Knock back the pizza dough and turn out onto a lightly floured surface. Knead for 1 minute, then divide the dough in half. Roll each portion into a ball, then flatten slightly. Using a floured rolling pin, roll out each portion to a 25 cm (10 inch) round. Place the rounds on the pizza trays. Cover with a clean cloth and set aside.

Place the radicchio on a baking tray. Drizzle with 1 tablespoon of the olive oil and season with sea salt. Bake for 5 minutes, then turn and bake for a further 5 minutes. Remove from the oven and allow to cool slightly, then remove the core and roughly chop.

In a small bowl, combine the remaining olive oil, honey, garlic and rosemary. Brush the mixture over the pizza bases. Arrange the radicchio, pear, walnuts and parmesan over the top, then drizzle with a little more olive oil.

Bake for 12–15 minutes, or until the bases are crisp and golden.

To serve, drizzle with the balsamic glaze and place a few rocket or extra torn radicchio leaves in the centre of each pizza. Cut the pizzas into quarters and serve.

Balsamic glaze is simply balsamic vinegar that has been simmered down and reduced to a thick, rich syrup. You can buy it in jars or bottles from gourmet food stores. To make your own, bring 250 ml (9 fl oz/1 cup) balsamic vinegar to the boil in a small saucepan, then reduce the heat and simmer for 20 minutes, or until thick enough to coat the back of a spoon. Remove from heat and allow to cool; any leftovers can be refrigerated in an airtight container for several weeks.

Mexican bean casserole on cornbread with avocado salsa

Leftover cornbread can be kept in an airtight container for up to one day. It can be sliced and frozen for up to four months. Thaw at room temperature. Cornbread is also delicious toasted.

2 tablespoons olive oil
1 brown onion, finely chopped
1 red capsicum (pepper), diced
1 green capsicum (pepper), diced
3 garlic cloves, crushed
1 teaspoon ground cumin
1 teaspoon dried oregano
440 g (15½ oz) tin kidney beans, rinsed
   and drained
440 g (15½ oz) tin chopped tomatoes
a pinch of cayenne pepper
½ teaspoon chilli flakes
250 ml (9 fl oz/1 cup) vegetable stock
1 small handful flat-leaf (Italian)
   parsley leaves, chopped
2 tablespoons lemon juice
sour cream, to serve (optional)

Cornbread

60 g (2¼ oz) unsalted butter, melted,
   plus extra, for greasing
150 g (5½ oz/1 cup) plain
   (all-purpose) flour
1 tablespoon baking powder
¼ teaspoon salt
1 teaspoon ground cumin
190 g (6¾ oz/1 cup) cornmeal (polenta)
60 g (2¼ oz/½ cup) finely grated
   cheddar cheese
2 eggs
250 ml (9 fl oz/1 cup) buttermilk

Avocado salsa

2 firm, ripe avocados, coarsely diced
2½ tablespoons lemon juice
½ red onion, finely diced
2 tablespoons chopped coriander (cilantro)
¼ teaspoon Tabasco sauce, or to taste

Heat the olive oil in a large heavy-based saucepan over medium heat. Add the onion and cook, stirring, for 5–8 minutes, or until softened. Add the capsicum and cook, stirring often, for a further 5 minutes, or until the capsicum starts to soften. Stir in the garlic, cumin and oregano and cook for 1 minute. Add the kidney beans, tomato, cayenne pepper, chilli flakes and stock and season to taste with sea salt and freshly ground black pepper. Bring the mixture to the boil, then reduce the heat to low and simmer for 30 minutes, stirring occasionally. Stir in the parsley and lemon juice and cook for a final 5 minutes. Adjust the seasoning if necessary.

Meanwhile, prepare the cornbread. Preheat the oven to 180°C (350°F/Gas 4) and grease an 18 cm (7 inch) springform cake tin with melted butter.

Sift the flour, baking powder, salt and cumin into a large bowl, then stir in the cornmeal and cheese. In another bowl, whisk together the eggs, buttermilk and melted butter. Pour the egg mixture into the dry ingredients and quickly stir until just combined; do not overmix the batter or the bread will be heavy. Spoon the batter into the springform tin, smooth the surface and bake for 35–40 minutes, or until the bread is golden and a skewer inserted into the middle comes out clean. Remove from the oven and stand in the tin on a wire rack for 10 minutes before removing.

Put the avocado salsa ingredients in a bowl and gently toss together. Season to taste.

Cut the warm cornbread into wedges and place on serving plates. Spoon the bean casserole over and top with the avocado salsa. Add a dollop of sour cream if desired and serve.

Preparation time: 30 minutes
plus 10 minutes standing

Cooking time: 1 hour
5 minutes

Serves: 4

Preparation time: 20 minutes　　**Cooking time:** 45 minutes　　**Serves:** 4

Eggplant curry

400 ml (14 fl oz) tin coconut cream
9 Japanese eggplants (aubergines),
   about 700 g (1 lb 9 oz), cut into
   2 cm (¾ inch)-thick rounds
1 teaspoon ground turmeric
2 tablespoons peanut oil
400 g (14 oz) tin chopped tomatoes
6 kaffir lime leaves, finely shredded,
   plus extra, to garnish
2 tablespoons soy sauce
1 tablespoon finely grated palm
   sugar (jaggery)
steamed rice, to serve
lime wedges, to serve

Curry paste
3 garlic cloves, chopped
3 red Asian shallots, chopped
2–4 small red chillies, or to taste, seeded
   and chopped
2 lemongrass stems, white part only,
   finely chopped
1 tablespoon coarsely grated or finely
   chopped fresh ginger
4 coriander (cilantro) roots, finely chopped

Combine the curry paste ingredients in a food processor or blender and process until a smooth paste forms, adding a little water if needed.

Place 200 ml (7 fl oz) of the coconut cream in a wok over low heat. Bring to a simmer and cook for 10 minutes, or until the oil starts to separate out. Increase the heat to medium, add the curry paste and cook for 5 minutes, or until aromatic. Transfer the mixture to a small bowl and set aside. Wipe the wok clean.

Place the eggplant in a large bowl, add the turmeric and toss to coat. Reheat the wok over high heat and add the oil. When the oil is hot, add the eggplant and stir-fry for 4–5 minutes, or until browned and softened.

Add the curry mixture and cook, stirring, for a further 2 minutes, or until aromatic. Stir in the tomato, lime leaves and remaining coconut cream, then cover and simmer for 15 minutes, or until the eggplant is very tender.

Remove the lid. Stir in the soy sauce and palm sugar and simmer, stirring occasionally, for 1–2 minutes, or until the sugar has dissolved.

Serve the curry on a bed of steamed rice, garnished with extra shredded lime leaves, and with lime wedges on the side.

Red Asian shallots are small, reddish-purple onions that grow in bulbs, and are sold in segments that look like large garlic cloves. They have a thin, papery skin and a concentrated flavour, and are easy to slice and grind. If unavailable, you can substitute French shallots (eschallots), or red or brown onion. To make this meal more substantial, a handful of toasted cashews or other nuts could be scattered over just before serving, to round out the protein.

Baked wholemeal crepes with asparagus and leek and basil cream

To prepare leeks for cooking, rinse them under cold running water to wash off any large clumps of dirt, then remove any tough dark green outer leaves and cut off the green ends. Without cutting through the root, cut the leeks lengthways into quarters. Fan the leaves out under running water and rinse well to release any sand or grit. Finally, cut off the fibrous root and slice as required.

16 asparagus spears, trimmed
130 g (4½ oz/1 cup) grated
    gruyère cheese
mixed leaf salad, to serve

Crepe batter
75 g (2½ oz/½ cup) wholemeal
    (whole-wheat) flour
75 g (2½ oz/½ cup) plain
    (all-purpose) flour
2 eggs, lightly beaten
375 ml (13 fl oz/1½ cups) milk

Leek and basil cream
40 g (1½ oz) butter
3 leeks, white part only, rinsed well
    and sliced
½ teaspoon freshly grated nutmeg
250 g (9 oz/1 cup) crème fraîche or
    sour cream
1 bunch (125 g/4½ oz) basil, leaves
    picked and finely chopped

To make the crepe batter, sift the flours and a pinch of sea salt into a bowl, returning any wholemeal flour solids to the mixture. Make a well in the centre. Add the eggs and milk to the well then gradually whisk in the flour until the batter is smooth. Cover and leave to stand for 30 minutes.

To make the leek and basil cream, melt the butter in a heavy-based saucepan over medium heat, then stir in the leek, nutmeg and 1 tablespoon water. Season to taste with sea salt and freshly ground black pepper, cover the pan, reduce the heat to low and cook for 40 minutes, or until the leek is very soft. Remove from the heat and allow to cool slightly, then stir in the crème fraîche and basil, and season to taste.

While the leek is cooking, preheat the oven to 180°C (350°F/Gas 4). Heat a non-stick 15 cm (6 inch) crepe pan over medium heat. Spoon 80 ml (2½ fl oz/⅓ cup) of the crepe batter into the pan, swirling the pan so the mixture covers the base. Cook for 1–2 minutes, or until the edges of the batter start to lift from the pan. Carefully turn the crepe over and cook the other side for 1–2 minutes, then transfer to a plate. Cook the remaining batter to make eight crepes.

Meanwhile, bring a saucepan of water to the boil. Add the asparagus and cook for 4–5 minutes, or until tender. Plunge into a bowl of iced water, then drain well and set aside.

Place about 60 ml (2 fl oz/¼ cup) of the leek mixture and two asparagus spears down the centre of each crepe, then roll up to enclose the filling. Place the crepes in a single layer, seam side down, in a 15 x 30 cm (6 x 12 inch) baking dish. Sprinkle with the gruyère and bake for 10–12 minutes, or until the cheese has melted and the crepes are warmed through. Serve hot, with the mixed leaf salad.

✳ **Preparation time:** 20 minutes
plus 30 minutes standing

✳ **Cooking time:**
1 hour 15 minutes

✳ **Serves:** 4
(makes 8)

Preparation time: 25 minutes

Cooking time:
1 hour 20 minutes

Serves: 4–6

Persian vegetable and fruit stew

2 tablespoons vegetable oil

2 brown onions, finely chopped

3 garlic cloves, finely chopped

2 celery stalks, finely chopped

2 carrots, sliced into 2 cm
(¾ inch)-thick rounds

400 g (14 oz) kipfler (fingerling) or other
waxy potatoes, scrubbed and sliced into
2 cm (¾ inch)-thick rounds

1 turnip (about 350 g/12 oz), peeled and
cut into 2 cm (¾ inch) cubes

2 large granny smith apples, peeled,
cored and chopped

2 teaspoons ground turmeric

1 handful flat-leaf (Italian)
parsley, chopped

1 handful coriander (cilantro) leaves,
chopped, plus extra, to garnish

100 g (3½ oz/½ cup) pitted prunes,
chopped

100 g (3½ oz/½ cup) dried apricots,
chopped

1.25 litres (44 fl oz/5 cups) vegetable
stock, approximately

Saffron rice

30 g (1 oz) butter

400 g (14 oz/2 cups) basmati rice, rinsed
well and drained

a large pinch of saffron threads

Heat the oil in a large flameproof casserole dish over medium heat. Add the onion, garlic and celery and cook, stirring, for 10–15 minutes, or until the celery is tender.

Add the carrot, potato, turnip, apple, turmeric and herbs and cook for 2 minutes, then add the prunes and apricots and enough of the stock to just cover the mixture. Bring to the boil, cover and reduce the heat to a gentle simmer. Cook for 40 minutes, then remove the lid and cook for a further 10–20 minutes, or until the vegetables are tender and the stew is rich and thick. Season to taste with sea salt and freshly ground black pepper.

Meanwhile, make the saffron rice. Melt the butter in a saucepan over medium heat. Add the rice and saffron and cook, stirring, for 2–3 minutes, or until the rice is heated through. Add 750 ml (26 fl oz/3 cups) water and quickly bring just to a simmer, then cover, reduce the heat to low and cook for 12 minutes, or until the water is absorbed. Remove from the heat and leave to stand, covered, for 5 minutes, then fluff the grains up with a fork.

Divide the rice among serving bowls and spoon the stew over. Garnish with the extra coriander and serve.

The thread-like stigma of a violet crocus, saffron is the world's most expensive spice because of the painstakingly delicate work involved in extracting it. Thankfully only a small amount is needed to impart its vivid colour and subtle flavour to food. The colour and flavour vary greatly according to its quality; less expensive brands are often adulterated with dyes.

This stew will freeze well for up to 1 month in an airtight container.

White bean and silverbeet timbales with roast tomato sauce

These timbales make a lovely light meal. Serve them with roasted vegetables such as cauliflower and zucchini or a mixed salad.

Fontina cheese is a rich, semi-soft cow's milk cheese from the Italian alps with a mild, sweet, nutty flavour. It melts well and is also a great table cheese. In this recipe, as a substitute you could use gruyère, emmental, edam or gouda.

Timbales were originally small metal or porcelain serving dishes, but today they refer to plain, round, high-sided moulds and to dishes cooked in them.

2 desiree or other all-purpose potatoes (about 400 g/14 oz), peeled and coarsely chopped
1 bunch (1 kg/2 lb 4 oz) silverbeet (Swiss chard), stalks trimmed
400 g (14 oz) tin butterbeans (lima beans), rinsed and drained
2 garlic cloves, crushed
2 egg yolks
2 tablespoons lemon juice
finely grated rind of 1 lemon
60 ml (2 fl oz/¼ cup) olive oil
90 g (3¼ oz/¾ cup) grated fontina cheese
⅓ cup chopped flat-leaf (Italian) parsley

Roast tomato sauce
500 g (1 lb 2 oz) roma (plum) tomatoes, cut into wedges
2½ tablespoons extra virgin olive oil
1½ tablespoons sherry vinegar
a large pinch of sugar

Place the potato in a saucepan, cover with cold water and bring to the boil. Reduce the heat to a simmer and cook for 20 minutes, or until the potato is tender. Drain, mash well and set aside.

Preheat the oven to 180°C (350°F/Gas 4). Lightly grease four 250 ml (9 fl oz/1 cup) timbale moulds or ramekins.

To prepare the timbales, place the silverbeet leaves in a large bowl and cover with boiling water. Drain well, then squeeze out the excess liquid and pat dry with paper towels. Line the base and side of each mould with the largest leaves, leaving the leaves overhanging to cover the timbales. Coarsely chop any remaining silverbeet.

Place the beans, garlic, egg yolks, lemon juice and lemon rind in a food processor and process for 30 seconds. Drizzle in the olive oil and continue to blend until a coarse paste forms. Transfer to a large bowl and add the potato, cheese, parsley and any chopped silverbeet. Mix together well and season to taste with sea salt and freshly ground black pepper.

Spoon the mixture into the timbales and fold the overhanging leaves over the top to enclose. Place on a baking tray.

To make the roast tomato sauce, place the tomatoes in a large roasting tin and drizzle with 1½ tablespoons of the olive oil. Season well with sea salt and freshly ground black pepper. Roast for 35 minutes.

Add the timbales to the oven and bake with the tomatoes for a further 15 minutes. Remove the tomatoes and timbales from the oven. Allow the timbales to stand for 5 minutes while finishing the sauce.

Transfer the tomatoes to a food processor, then add the vinegar, sugar and remaining olive oil and process until smooth.

Turn the timbales out from their moulds and serve with the roast tomato sauce.

Preparation time: 20 minutes   **Cooking time:** 1 hour 15 minutes   **Serves:** 4

Preparation time: 20 minutes **Cooking time:** 35 minutes **Serves:** 4

Green vegetable curry

1 tablespoon vegetable oil
2 tablespoons vegetarian Thai green
  curry paste
350 ml (12 fl oz) coconut milk
2 potatoes, peeled and cut into 2 cm
  (¾ inch) cubes
3 Japanese eggplants (aubergines),
  cut into 2 cm (¾ inch)-thick rounds
½ butternut pumpkin (squash), about
  400 g (14 oz), peeled and cut into
  2 cm (¾ inch) cubes
1 small sweet potato (about 400 g/14 oz),
  peeled and cut into 2 cm (¾ inch) cubes
7 kaffir lime leaves, 5 torn and
  2 finely shredded
1 tablespoon soy sauce
1 tablespoon lime juice
40 g (1½ oz/¼ cup) cashew nuts, toasted
  and coarsely chopped
1 small handful coriander (cilantro) leaves
1 small handful mint leaves, shredded
steamed jasmine rice, to serve

Heat the oil in a wok over medium heat. Add the curry paste and cook, stirring, for 2–3 minutes, or until fragrant. Pour in the coconut milk and stir until thoroughly combined. Simmer for 3 minutes, or until the oil starts to separate out.

Add the potato and eggplant to the wok and cook, stirring occasionally, for 10 minutes. Add the pumpkin and sweet potato and cook for a further 10 minutes, or until all the vegetables are tender.

Add the torn lime leaves, soy sauce and lime juice and heat through.

Ladle the curry into serving bowls. Garnish with the cashews, coriander, mint and shredded lime leaves and serve with steamed jasmine rice.

Many Thai curry pastes contain shrimp paste, so check the label carefully if you prefer to avoid eating it.

Kaffir lime leaves (also called 'makrut') add a citrus tang to curries and other dishes. Remove the coarse central vein from the leaves before tearing or shredding them. They are available from supermarkets and Asian grocery stores; any leftover leaves can be frozen in airtight plastic bags for later use.

Clay pot mushrooms, tofu and vermicelli

Mung bean vermicelli (also known as cellophane noodles, glass noodles or bean thread noodles) are made from ground mung beans. They are sold in dried form and are thin, white and quite brittle, but become slippery and translucent once soaked.

Tofu puffs are cubes of tofu that have been deep-fried until puffed and golden.

Vegetarian oyster sauce is made from mushrooms rather than oysters, but has a traditional Asian flavour that vegetarians can enjoy. Soy sauce can be substituted. You'll find these ingredients in Asian grocery stores and some supermarkets.

10 dried shiitake mushrooms
50 g (1 ¾ oz) mung bean vermicelli
18 tofu puffs
2 garlic cloves, finely chopped
2 cm (¾ inch) piece of fresh ginger, peeled and cut into thin shreds
250 g (9 oz) Chinese cabbage (wong bok), thinly sliced
200 g (7 oz) oyster mushrooms
2 star anise
250 ml (9 fl oz/1 cup) vegetable stock
150 ml (5 fl oz) vegetarian oyster sauce
2 tablespoons soy sauce
4 spring onions (scallions), thinly sliced on the diagonal
1 tablespoon cornflour (cornstarch)
½ teaspoon sesame oil
steamed rice, to serve

Put the mushrooms in a heatproof bowl and pour in 250 ml (9 fl oz/1 cup) water. Leave to soak for 30 minutes. Meanwhile, place the vermicelli in a large bowl, cover with warm water and soak for 15 minutes, or until soft.

Preheat the oven to 180°C (350°F/Gas 4).

Drain the mushrooms, reserving the soaking liquid. Trim the stalks from the mushrooms, then cut the caps into quarters and place in a clay pot or ovenproof saucepan with the reserved soaking liquid.

Drain the noodles well, then add to the shiitake mushrooms, along with the tofu, garlic, ginger, cabbage, oyster mushrooms, star anise, stock and half the oyster sauce. Cover and bake for 35 minutes.

Stir in the soy sauce, remaining oyster sauce and spring onion, then cover and bake for a further 15 minutes. Remove from the oven and place on the stovetop over low heat.

Mix the cornflour with 2 tablespoons water to form a smooth paste. Stir the mixture through the noodles and cook, stirring, for 3–5 minutes, or until the sauce has boiled and thickened.

Divide among serving bowls and drizzle with the sesame oil. Serve with steamed rice.

Preparation time: 10 minutes
plus 30 minutes soaking

Cooking time: 55 minutes

Serves: 4

Preparation time: 45 minutes
plus 1 hour chilling

Cooking time: 50 minutes

Serves: 4

Greek red lentil and potato rissoles

2 potatoes (about 380 g/13½ oz), peeled and chopped
400 g (14 oz/1⅔ cups) red lentils
2 tablespoons olive oil
1 small fennel bulb (about 250 g/9 oz), trimmed, tough core removed, then finely chopped
1 brown onion, finely chopped
2 garlic cloves, crushed
40 g (1½ oz/¼ cup) pitted kalamata olives, coarsely chopped
45 g (1½ oz/⅓ cup) chopped semi-dried (sun-blushed) tomatoes
75 g (2½ oz/½ cup) crumbled feta cheese
1 handful flat-leaf (Italian) parsley, chopped
1 handful mint leaves, chopped
2 eggs
1 tablespoon milk
75 g (2½ oz/½ cup) plain (all-purpose) flour
180 g (6 oz/2¼ cups) fresh breadcrumbs, lightly toasted
125 ml (4 fl oz/½ cup) vegetable oil
sea salt, to sprinkle
lemon wedges, to serve

Place the potato in a small saucepan, cover with cold water and bring to the boil over medium–high heat. Cook for 15–20 minutes, or until the potato is tender. Drain, mash well and set aside.

Meanwhile, rinse the lentils under cold running water, then drain. Place in a saucepan of lightly salted water and bring to the boil. Reduce the heat to low and simmer gently for 20–30 minutes, or until tender. Drain well and set aside.

Heat the olive oil in a heavy-based frying pan over medium–low heat. Add the fennel, onion and garlic and cook, stirring, for 10–15 minutes, or until the fennel is tender. Transfer to a large bowl and allow to cool.

Add the mashed potato and lentils to the fennel mixture, along with the olives, tomato, feta, parsley and mint. Season to taste with sea salt and freshly ground black pepper and mix until well combined. Form into 12 rissoles, using about ⅓ cup of mixture at a time, and place on a tray. Cover and refrigerate for 1 hour.

In a small bowl, whisk together the eggs and milk. Place the flour and breadcrumbs in two separate shallow bowls. Coat the rissoles in the flour, dip them in the egg, allowing the excess to run off, then finally coat them in the breadcrumbs.

Heat half the oil in a large heavy-based frying pan over medium heat. Working in batches, and adding the remaining oil as needed, cook the rissoles for 2–3 minutes on each side, or until golden and warmed through.

Drain on paper towels, then sprinkle with sea salt and serve with lemon wedges.

Serve these rissoles with a salad of shaved fennel, thinly sliced red onions, capers and watercress bound lightly with a good egg mayonnaise. Red lentils are small and a vibrant orange colour. They don't require pre-soaking and break down easily when cooked. They are used to help thicken dals and pâtés and are great in soups.

Green vegetable bake with pine nut and pecorino crumble

You can use thawed frozen peas instead of fresh podded peas. Add them to the bowl of sautéed vegetables with the ricotta and cream.

Pecorino is a hard, strongly flavoured cheese made from sheep's milk. It is quite similar to parmesan cheese in flavour and is one of Italy's most popular cheeses.

155 g (5½ oz/1 cup) fresh shelled peas
    (about 375 g/13 oz unshelled peas)
1 large fennel bulb, trimmed,
    tough core removed, then cut into
    2 cm (¾ inch) pieces
40 g (1½ oz) butter
2 bunches (600 g/1 lb 5 oz) English
    spinach, tough stems removed, leaves
    washed and dried
2 tablespoons olive oil
2 zucchini (courgettes), sliced into
    2 cm (¾ inch)-thick rounds
1 teaspoon finely grated lemon rind
2 tablespoons lemon juice
¼ cup chopped dill
1 tablespoon chopped flat-leaf
    (Italian) parsley
250 g (9 oz/1 cup) ricotta cheese
150 ml (5 fl oz) thick cream

Crumble topping
2 teaspoons fennel seeds
100 g (3½ oz/1 cup) grated
    pecorino cheese
40 g (1½ oz/¼ cup) pine nuts,
    coarsely chopped
80 g (2¾ oz/1 cup) fresh breadcrumbs
20 g (¾ oz) unsalted butter, chopped

Preheat the oven to 190°C (375°F/Gas 5). Grease a 2 litre (70 fl oz/8 cup) baking dish.

Bring a large saucepan of salted water to the boil. Add the peas and cook for 5 minutes, or until just tender. Using a slotted spoon, remove the peas to a large bowl. Add the fennel to the boiling water and cook for 5–6 minutes, or until just tender. Drain well, then pat dry with paper towels and set aside.

Melt half the butter in a large non-stick frying pan over medium heat. Add the spinach and cook, stirring occasionally, for 2–3 minutes, or until the spinach has wilted and the liquid has almost evaporated. Drain very well, then transfer to the bowl with the peas.

Return the frying pan to the heat and melt the remaining butter with 1 tablespoon of the olive oil. Add the blanched fennel and cook for 2 minutes on each side, or until golden brown; transfer to the bowl with the spinach. Heat the remaining oil in the pan, then add the zucchini and cook for 2 minutes on each side, or until golden; transfer to the bowl.

Add the lemon rind, lemon juice, herbs, ricotta and cream to the sautéed vegetables and gently toss until well coated. Season to taste with sea salt and freshly ground black pepper. Spread the vegetable mixture in the baking dish.

To make the crumble mixture, combine the fennel seeds, pecorino, pine nuts and breadcrumbs in a bowl. Sprinkle the crumble mixture over the vegetables and scatter the butter over the top.

Bake for 20–25 minutes, or until bubbling and golden. Serve hot.

Preparation time: 30 minutes   **Cooking time:** 55 minutes   **Serves:** 4–6

Preparation time: 30 minutes   **Cooking time:** 30 minutes   **Serves:** 4

Mushroom and spinach lasagne

60 ml (2 fl oz/¼ cup) olive oil
60 g (2¼ oz) unsalted butter
300 g (10½ oz) large portobello or field
  mushrooms, thinly sliced
200 g (7 oz) Swiss brown mushrooms,
  thickly sliced
100 g (3½ oz) oyster mushrooms
150 g (5½ oz) shimeji or enoki
  mushrooms, separated
200 g (7 oz) baby spinach leaves
3 garlic cloves, crushed
100 ml (3½ fl oz) verjuice
100 ml (3½ fl oz) vegetable stock
200 g (7 oz) crème fraîche or sour cream
100 g (3½ oz) gorgonzola
  cheese, crumbled
1 small handful marjoram, plus extra,
  to garnish
4 fresh lasagne sheets (each about
  10 x 14 cm/4 x 5½ inches)
30 g (1 oz/¼ cup) chopped
  roasted hazelnuts

Heat the oil and butter in a large non-stick frying pan over medium–high heat. Reserving the enoki mushrooms, sauté all the other mushrooms for 5 minutes, or until browned and softened. Add the enoki mushrooms, baby spinach and garlic and cook for 1 minute. Stir in the verjuice and stock and bring to the boil, then reduce the heat to low. Stir in the crème fraîche, gorgonzola and marjoram. Simmer over medium heat for 1 minute, or until reduced to a light sauce consistency. Season to taste with sea salt and freshly ground black pepper.

Bring two large saucepans of salted water to the boil. Cut each sheet of lasagne widthways into three even-sized squares or rectangles. Cook the pasta in the boiling water for 3–4 minutes, or until al dente. Drain.

Place a lasagne sheet portion on each serving plate. Spoon one third of the spinach and mushrooms over the top. Add another lasagne sheet portion to each and top with half of the remaining spinach and mushrooms. Arrange the remaining pasta over the top and spoon over the remaining spinach and mushrooms.

Sprinkle with the hazelnuts, garnish with the extra marjoram and serve.

Not quite as tart as lemon juice or vinegar, verjuice is the juice of unripe grapes, although it can also be made from other fruit such as crab apples or gooseberries. If you don't have any you could use a dry white wine in this dish.

Kung pao with broccoli and peanuts

A classic spicy stir-fry dish from the Sichuan province of China, kung pao traditionally features chicken, vegetables and peanuts or cashew nuts, and most importantly sichuan peppercorns — the dried red berries of the prickly ash tree, native to Sichuan. The peppercorns have a spicy-hot flavour and a distinctive numbing effect on the palate.

270 g (9½ oz/1⅓ cups) long-grain white rice
2½ tablespoons peanut oil
4 garlic cloves, very thinly sliced
1½ tablespoons thinly sliced fresh ginger
2 long red chillies, thinly sliced on the diagonal
3 teaspoons sichuan peppercorns
600 g (1 lb 5 oz) broccoli, cut into florets, the larger ones cut in half
200 g (7 oz) mixed Asian mushrooms, such as enoki and shiitake, trimmed, and any large ones cut in half
2 tablespoons light soy sauce
3 teaspoons Chinese black rice vinegar
3 teaspoons caster (superfine) sugar
1½ teaspoons sesame oil
270 g (9½ oz) tin sliced water chestnuts, drained
110 g (3¾ oz/⅔ cup) roasted unsalted peanuts
4 spring onions (scallions), cut into 4 cm (1½ inch) lengths

Place the rice in a saucepan with 500 ml (17 fl oz/2 cups) water. Cover and bring to the boil, then immediately turn the heat down very low and simmer gently for 12 minutes, or until tender. Remove from the heat. Keeping the lid on, leave the rice to stand for 10 minutes.

While the rice is standing, heat a wok over high heat. Add the peanut oil and swirl to coat the side. Add the garlic, ginger, chilli and peppercorns and stir-fry for 30 seconds, or until aromatic.

Add the broccoli and stir-fry for 2 minutes, then add the mushrooms and stir-fry for 1–2 minutes, or until the mushrooms are tender.

Add the soy sauce, vinegar, sugar, sesame oil and water chestnuts. Toss until well combined and heated through.

Finally add the peanuts and spring onion and stir for 30 seconds, or until the spring onion has just turned bright green, but has not collapsed.

Serve immediately, with the steamed rice.

Preparation time: 15 minutes   **Cooking time:** 25 minutes   **Serves:** 4

Preparation time: 15 minutes
+ 30 minutes soaking

Cooking time: 45 minutes

Serves: 4

Fettuccine with roast fennel, saffron, olives and breadcrumbs

a large pinch of saffron threads
60 ml (2 fl oz/¼ cup) white wine
4 fennel bulbs, trimmed, tough cores
  removed, then thinly sliced
2 red onions, halved and thinly sliced
4 garlic cloves, finely chopped
125 ml (4 fl oz/½ cup) olive oil
80 g (2¾ oz) day-old sourdough bread,
  crusts removed
500 g (1 lb 2 oz) fresh fettuccine
80 g (2¾ oz/½ cup) pitted kalamata
  olives, sliced
40 g (1½ oz/¼ cup) toasted pine nuts
1½ tablespoons chopped oregano
¼ cup chopped flat-leaf (Italian) parsley
1 small handful baby rocket (arugula)
shaved parmesan cheese, to serve
  (optional)

Preheat the oven to 180°C (350°F/Gas 4).

Put the saffron in a small bowl, pour in the wine and leave to soak for 30 minutes.

Place the fennel, onion and garlic in a baking dish. Drizzle with 80 ml (2½ fl oz/⅓ cup) of the olive oil and toss to coat. Bake for 45 minutes, or until the fennel is golden and tender.

Reduce the oven temperature to 120°C (235°F/Gas ½). Add the saffron and wine to the fennel and onion mixture, then return to the oven to keep warm.

Meanwhile, put the bread in a food processor and pulse until coarse crumbs form. Heat the remaining olive oil in a heavy-based frying pan, add the breadcrumbs and stir over medium–low heat for 5–6 minutes, or until crisp and golden. Drain on paper towels and set aside.

Bring a large saucepan of salted water to the boil. Add the fettuccine and cook for 3–4 minutes, or until al dente. Drain well, then return the pasta to the saucepan.

Add the fennel mixture to the saucepan with the olives, pine nuts, herbs, rocket and breadcrumbs. Toss well to combine.

Divide the pasta among serving bowls. Serve scattered with parmesan shavings if desired.

Dry potato curry with egg and peas

Garam masala is a blend of ground spices — typically including black pepper, mace, cloves, cumin, coriander, cinnamon, cardamom and fennel — that is widely used in Indian cooking to enhance spicy dishes. It is available from supermarkets.
If you like your curry extra spicy, add 2 chopped or sliced bird's eye chillies when adding the green chilli.

4 eggs
220 g (7¾ oz/1 cup) brown rice
1 tablespoon vegetable oil
2 teaspoons brown mustard seeds
40 g (1½ oz) butter
2 brown onions, thinly sliced
2 garlic cloves, chopped
2 teaspoons grated fresh ginger
1 green chilli, chopped
2 teaspoons ground turmeric
1 teaspoon ground cumin
1 teaspoon garam masala
750 g (1 lb 10 oz) waxy potatoes, peeled and cut into 3 cm (1¼ inch) chunks
100 g (3½ oz/⅔ cup) frozen peas, thawed
2 tablespoons lemon juice
1 small handful mint leaves
2 tablespoons mango chutney

Mint and ginger raita
125 g (4½ oz/½ cup) Greek-style yoghurt
1 Lebanese (short) cucumber, peeled, seeds removed and coarsely grated
1 garlic clove, crushed
½ teaspoon grated fresh ginger
1 small handful mint leaves, finely chopped

To make the mint and ginger raita, place all the ingredients in a small bowl. Mix together well and season to taste with sea salt. Cover and refrigerate until serving time.

Bring a small saucepan of cold water to the boil over medium heat. Add the eggs, reduce the heat to low and simmer for 10 minutes. Remove the eggs and place in a bowl of cold water until cooled. Drain the eggs, then peel, cut into halves and set aside.

Place the rice in a saucepan. Add 750 ml (26 fl oz/3 cups) water and bring to a simmer. Cook, adding more water if necessary, for 20–30 minutes, or until tender. Drain well, cover and keep warm

Meanwhile, heat the oil in a frying pan. Add the mustard seeds and cook over medium heat until the seeds start to pop. Reduce the heat to low, then add the butter and onion and cook, stirring, for 5 minutes, or until the onion has softened. Add the garlic, ginger, chilli, spices and potato, stirring to coat in the spice mix. Pour in 125 ml (4 fl oz/½ cup) water, then cover and simmer over low heat for 25 minutes, or until the potato is just tender.

Stir in the peas and lemon juice and cook for 3 minutes, or until the peas are heated through. Stir in the mint and season to taste with sea salt and freshly ground black pepper.

Divide the rice among serving plates or bowls. Top with the curry and garnish with the egg halves. Serve topped with a dollop of the mint and ginger raita, with the mango chutney on the side.

Preparation time: 25 minutes   **Cooking time:** 45 minutes   **Serves:** 4

Preparation time: 25 minutes
plus 2 hours chilling

Cooking time:
1 hour 10 minutes

Serves: 4

Puy lentils with chestnuts and spinach on soft polenta

200 g (7 oz) frozen peeled chestnuts, or
    400 g (14 oz) fresh chestnuts, peeled
2 tablespoons olive oil
1 small fennel bulb, trimmed, tough cores
    removed, then thinly sliced
1 celery stalk, thinly sliced
2 garlic cloves
2 tablespoons thyme, chopped,
    plus extra, to garnish
1 tablespoon tomato paste
    (concentrated purée)
375 g (13 oz/2 cups) puy lentils
1 bay leaf
2 vine-ripened tomatoes, chopped
185 ml (6 fl oz/¾ cup) white wine
750 ml (26 fl oz/3 cups) vegetable stock
80 g (2¾ oz/1¾ cups) baby spinach leaves
1 small handful flat-leaf (Italian) parsley,
    coarsely chopped

Polenta

500 ml (17 fl oz/2 cups) vegetable stock
500 ml (17 fl oz/2 cups) milk
½ teaspoon sea salt
175 g (6 oz) polenta
100 g (3½ oz) taleggio cheese, chopped
60 ml (2 fl oz/¼ cup) cream

Cook the chestnuts in a saucepan of salted boiling water for 4 minutes. Drain well, then cut into quarters and set aside.

Heat the olive oil in a heavy-based saucepan over medium–low heat. Add the fennel, celery, garlic and thyme. Cook, stirring, for 8–10 minutes, or until the vegetables have softened and caramelised slightly. Stir in the tomato paste and cook for 30 seconds.

Stir in the lentils, bay leaf and tomato, then pour in the wine and stock. Increase the heat to medium and bring to the boil, then reduce the heat to low, cover and simmer for 30 minutes.

Add the chestnuts, then cover and cook for a further 20 minutes, or until the lentils are tender. Stir in the baby spinach and parsley and cook for 2–3 minutes, or until the spinach has wilted. Remove from the heat, season to taste with sea salt and freshly ground black pepper, and keep warm.

While the lentils are simmering, make the polenta. Bring the stock and milk to the boil in a heavy-based saucepan over high heat. Stir in the salt and reduce the heat to medium–low. Gradually add the polenta in a thin steady stream, whisking constantly until smooth. Cook, stirring constantly, for 15 minutes, or until the polenta is very thick and pulls away from the side of the pan. Remove from the heat and stir in the taleggio and cream until combined. Season to taste.

Divide the polenta among serving bowls and spoon the lentil mixture over. Garnish with extra thyme and serve.

To peel fresh chestnuts, see page 49. Puy lentils are small blue-green lentils from the Puy region of France. They hold their shape well during cooking and are available from delicatessens.

Taleggio is a semi-soft Italian washed-rind cheese with a strong aroma but surprisingly mild flavour, with an almost fruity tang; it has a buttery texture and melts well. As a substitute you could use fontina or a good parmesan in the polenta. This dish is not suitable for freezing.

Linguine with green beans, potato and mint and almond pesto

Instead of pecorino cheese in the mint and almond pesto, use parmesan if you prefer.

3 desiree or other all-purpose potatoes
  (about 400 g/14 oz), diced
200 g (7 oz) green beans, trimmed
  and cut into short lengths
400 g (14 oz) linguine
green salad, to serve

Mint and almond pesto
60 g (2¼ oz/⅓ cup) blanched almonds
1 garlic clove, sliced
25 g (1 oz/1¼ cups) mint leaves,
  lightly packed
1 small handful flat-leaf (Italian) parsley
125 ml (4 fl oz/½ cup) extra virgin olive oil
50 g (1¾ oz/½ cup) grated pecorino
  cheese, plus extra, to serve

Preheat the oven to 180°C (350°F/Gas 4).

To make the mint and almond pesto, spread the almonds on a baking tray and toast in the oven for 4–5 minutes, or until lightly toasted. Allow to cool, then transfer to a food processor with the garlic and blend until finely chopped. Add the mint, parsley and olive oil, and blend until well combined. Add the pecorino and pulse until just combined. Season to taste with sea salt and freshly ground black pepper, and set aside.

Bring a large saucepan of salted water to the boil. Add the potato and cook for 10 minutes, then add the beans and cook for a further 3 minutes, or until the vegetables are tender. Drain well.

Meanwhile, cook the pasta in another saucepan of boiling salted water until al dente, following the packet instructions. Drain well, reserving 2 tablespoons of the cooking water.

Return the hot pasta to the saucepan with the reserved cooking water. Add the potato, beans and mint and almond pesto, and toss together until well combined.

Divide among serving bowls. Serve scattered with extra grated pecorino, with a green salad on the side.

Preparation time: 15 minutes   **Cooking time:** 20 minutes   **Serves:** 4

✳ **Preparation time:** 35 minutes   ✳ **Cooking time:** 1 hour 10 minutes   ✳ **Serves:** 4

Polenta and provolone soufflés with red wine–rosemary capsicum

100 g (3½ oz) butter
75 g (2½ oz/1 cup) finely grated
  provolone cheese
500 ml (17 fl oz/2 cups) milk
90 g (3¼ oz/½ cup) polenta
1 teaspoon sea salt
4 large eggs, separated, plus 2 extra
  egg whites
1½ teaspoons baking powder
2 tablespoons snipped chives

Red wine–rosemary capsicum
2 tablespoons extra virgin olive oil
2 red capsicums (peppers), chopped
½ tablespoon finely chopped rosemary
1 garlic clove, crushed
60 ml (2 fl oz/¼ cup) red wine

To make the red wine–rosemary capsicum, heat the olive oil in a heavy-based saucepan over medium–low heat. Add the capsicum, rosemary and garlic and cook, stirring, for 15–20 minutes, or until the capsicum has softened. Pour in the wine and cook for 5 minutes, or until the liquid has reduced and thickened slightly. Season to taste with sea salt and freshly ground black pepper, then remove from the heat and set aside.

Preheat the oven to 180°C (350°F/Gas 4). Melt 40 g (1½ oz) of the butter and use it to grease four 375 ml (13 fl oz/1½ cup) soufflé dishes. Sprinkle the dishes with 25 g (1 oz/¼ cup) of the provolone.

Bring the milk to the boil in a heavy-based saucepan over high heat. Gradually add the polenta in a thin steady stream, whisking constantly until smooth. Stir in the remaining butter and the salt and reduce the heat to medium–low. Cook, stirring constantly, for 10–15 minutes, or until the polenta is very thick and pulls away from the side of the pan. Remove from the heat and transfer to a large bowl.

Add the egg yolks, one at a time, to the polenta, mixing well after each addition. Add the baking powder, chives and another 25 g (1 oz/¼ cup) of the provolone and mix well.

Using electric beaters, whisk all the egg whites in a large bowl until firm peaks form. Add a large spoonful of the beaten egg white to the polenta, stirring it in to loosen the mixture, then gently fold in the remaining whites, taking care not to lose too much volume. Spoon the mixture into the soufflé dishes and place on a baking tray. Sprinkle with the remaining provolone and bake for 25–30 minutes, or until the soufflés have risen and are golden and firm to the touch.

Serve immediately, with the red wine–rosemary capsicum.

Often moulded into a pear shape, provolone is a golden Italian cheese with a glossy rind. The young cheese has a mild, delicate flavour, which sharpens with age. Instead of using provolone in the soufflés, parmesan, gruyère or cheddar cheese will also work well.

Once the egg whites have been beaten into firm peaks, don't let them sit too long before incorporating them into the polenta mixture or the air will deflate and the soufflés won't rise properly.

These soufflés are not suitable for freezing.

Cauliflower and white bean korma

This dish is quite versatile, so feel free to substitute other vegetables that are in season — broccoli, pumpkin (winter squash), green beans, potato and orange sweet potato will all work well.

60 ml (2 fl oz/¼ cup) peanut oil
500 g (1 lb 2 oz/4 cups) cauliflower florets
  (from about ½ head of cauliflower)
1 brown onion, finely chopped
4 vine-ripened tomatoes (about 500 g/
  1 lb 2 oz), finely chopped
100 ml (3½ fl oz) vegetable stock
12 curry leaves, plus extra, to garnish
120 g (4¼ oz/¾ cup) roasted cashew
  nuts, coarsely chopped
400 g (14 oz) tin white beans (such as
  cannellini), rinsed and drained
80 ml (2½ fl oz/⅓ cup) pouring cream
warmed naan bread, to serve
steamed basmati rice, to serve
lime pickle, to serve (optional)

Spice paste
3 garlic cloves, crushed
2 teaspoons grated fresh ginger
2 teaspoons garam masala
1 teaspoon ground turmeric
1 teaspoon ground cumin
1 teaspoon ground coriander
1 teaspoon chilli powder
1 teaspoon sea salt

Heat half the oil in a large heavy-based frying pan over medium–high heat. Add the cauliflower and cook, stirring, for 5 minutes, or until golden. Transfer the cauliflower to a plate.

Heat the remaining oil in the pan. Add the onion and cook over medium heat, stirring occasionally, for 8 minutes, or until softened.

Meanwhile, to make the spice paste, combine all the ingredients in a small food processor and blend until a paste forms.

Add the spice paste to the onion and cook, stirring, for 1 minute, or until aromatic.

Stir in the tomato, stock, curry leaves, cashews, beans and sautéed cauliflower. Bring to a simmer, then reduce the heat to low. Cover and cook for 10–15 minutes, or until the cauliflower is tender. Stir in the cream and cook for 1–2 minutes, or until heated through.

Ladle the curry into serving bowls and garnish with the extra curry leaves. Serve with naan bread and steamed rice, and lime pickle if desired.

Preparation time: 25 minutes   Cooking time: 35 minutes   Serves: 4

Preparation time: 30 minutes   **Cooking time:** 45 minutes   **Serves:** 4

Roasted pumpkin gnocchi with three-cheese sauce

1 kg (2 lb 4 oz) butternut pumpkin
  (squash), peeled and cut into
  1 cm (½ inch)-thick slices
1 tablespoon olive oil
350 g (12 oz/1⅓ cups) firm fresh ricotta
  cheese
1 egg yolk
110 g (3¾ oz/1 cup) finely grated
  parmesan cheese
100 g (3½ oz/⅔ cup) plain (all-purpose)
  flour, plus extra, for dusting
40 g (1½ oz) butter
50 g (1¾ oz/½ cup) toasted
  walnuts, chopped
finely grated rind of 1 lemon
thyme sprigs, to garnish

Three-cheese sauce
60 g (2¼ oz/¼ cup) firm ricotta cheese
60 g (2¼ oz/¼ cup) mascarpone cheese
40 g (1½ oz/⅓ cup) blue cheese, crumbled
2½ tablespoons milk

Preheat the oven to 200°C (400°F/Gas 6). Line two baking trays with baking paper.

Toss the pumpkin in the olive oil and spread on the baking trays. Sprinkle with sea salt and roast for 20 minutes. Then turn each piece over and roast for a further 20 minutes, or until most of the excess moisture has evaporated and the pumpkin is tender. Transfer to a bowl and mash until smooth, then set aside to cool.

Meanwhile, to make the three-cheese sauce, place all the ingredients in a food processor and pulse until well combined. Transfer to a saucepan and set aside.

Bring a large saucepan of salted water to the boil. Reduce the heat to a simmer, then cover the pan to stop the water evaporating.

Press the ricotta through a sieve, into the cooled pumpkin. Add the egg yolk and 25 g (1 oz/¼ cup) of the parmesan and mix until thoroughly combined. Season to taste with sea salt and freshly ground black pepper. Add the flour and mix until just combined; the mixture will be soft. Divide the mixture into four portions. Place one portion on a very lightly floured surface. Using your hands, roll it into a log 2 cm (¾ inch) in diameter, adding a little more flour if it sticks to the surface. Cut into 3 cm (1¼ inch)-long pieces and set aside. Repeat with the remaining mixture.

Melt the butter in a large saucepan over medium–low heat. Add half the gnocchi to the simmering pan of water. As soon as the gnocchi rise to the surface (after about 1 minute), remove them with a slotted spoon and gently toss to coat in the melted butter. Repeat with the remaining gnocchi.

Meanwhile, heat the three-cheese sauce over medium–low heat, stirring occasionally, until hot but not simmering. Divide the gnocchi among four warmed plates or shallow bowls. Spoon the sauce over, then scatter with the walnuts and lemon rind. Garnish with thyme and serve.

To warm plates for serving, heat them in a microwave oven for 30 seconds to 1 minute per plate. If the plates are decorated with metallic paint, immerse them in hot water until warmed instead, then wipe them dry.

Tofu burgers with sweet chilli mayonnaise

You can serve these burgers with sweet potato chips, as we have done. Cut 3 peeled orange sweet potatoes into batons 1 cm (½ inch) thick, then pat dry with paper towels to remove excess moisture. In a saucepan or deep-fryer, heat 5 cm (2 inches) oil over medium–high heat to 180°C (350°F), or until a cube of bread dropped into the oil browns in 15 seconds. Deep-fry the chips in batches for 5–8 minutes, or until golden and cooked through. Drain on paper towels before serving.

2 tablespoons vegetable oil
6 burger buns, split in half, toasted
1 Lebanese (short) cucumber, thinly sliced lengthways
100 g (3½ oz) bean sprouts, tails trimmed
½ red capsicum (pepper), very thinly sliced
sweet chilli sauce, to serve

Tofu patties

600 g (1 lb 5 oz) firm tofu, drained well
1 carrot, coarsely grated
3 garlic cloves, crushed
3 cm (1¼ inch) piece of fresh ginger, peeled and finely grated
2 tablespoons white miso paste
1 tablespoon soy sauce
1 egg, lightly beaten
2 tablespoons finely chopped coriander (cilantro) leaves
80 g (2¾ oz/½ cup) sesame seeds

Sweet chilli mayonnaise

125 g (4½ oz/½ cup) whole-egg mayonnaise
60 ml (2 fl oz/¼ cup) sweet chilli sauce

To make the tofu patties, coarsely grate the tofu into a large bowl. Using your hands, squeeze out and discard any excess liquid from the tofu. Add the remaining patty ingredients, except the sesame seeds, to the tofu and mix together well until the mixture holds its shape. Shape into six patties about 7.5 cm (3 inches) in diameter. Spread the sesame seeds on a plate and coat each patty with them, pressing them on firmly. Refrigerate the patties for 30 minutes, or until firm.

Meanwhile, to make the sweet chilli mayonnaise, place the ingredients in a small bowl and mix until well combined. Cover and refrigerate until serving time.

Heat the oil in a large non-stick frying pan over medium heat. Add the patties and cook for 3 minutes on each side, or until golden and heated through.

Place the burger bun bases on serving plates. Top with the patties, then add the cucumber, bean sprouts and capsicum. Add a dollop of the sweet chilli mayonnaise and a little sweet chilli sauce, top with the burger lids and serve immediately.

Preparation time: 20 minutes
plus 30 minutes chilling

Cooking time: 10 minutes

Serves: 6

Preparation time: 20 minutes

Cooking time:
1 hour 20 minutes

Serves: 6

Baked turlu turlu with haloumi

1 fennel bulb (about 450 g/1 lb), trimmed, tough cores removed, then cut into 2 cm (¾ inch) wedges
2 small carrots, quartered lengthways
1 yellow capsicum (pepper), cut into 1 cm (½ inch)-thick strips
1 red onion, cut into 2 cm (¾ inch) wedges
6 whole garlic cloves
2 teaspoons ground coriander
1 teaspoon chilli flakes
½ teaspoon ground allspice
1½ teaspoons sea salt
2½ tablespoons olive oil, plus extra, for drizzling
2 zucchini (courgettes), cut into 1 cm (½ inch)-thick rounds
1 tablespoon lemon juice
400 g (14 oz) tin chickpeas, rinsed and drained
250 g (9 oz) haloumi cheese, cut into 1 cm (½ inch)-thick slices
1 handful coarsely chopped flat-leaf (Italian) parsley
Greek-style yoghurt, to serve

Tomato sauce
1½ tablespoons olive oil
1 brown onion, finely chopped
2 garlic cloves, finely chopped
800 g (1 lb 12 oz) tin chopped tomatoes
1 teaspoon thyme leaves

Preheat the oven to 180°C (350°/Gas 4). Line two baking trays with baking paper, allowing the paper to overhang the edges a little.

In a large bowl, combine the fennel, carrot, capsicum, onion, garlic, spices, salt and the olive oil, tossing to coat the vegetables. Spread the vegetables on the baking trays, then cover tightly with foil and bake for 30 minutes. Remove and discard the foil. Add the zucchini to the baking trays and sprinkle with the lemon juice. Toss to combine, then bake for a further 25 minutes.

Remove the vegetables from the oven, toss gently again and add the chickpeas and haloumi. Drizzle with some extra olive oil and toss gently. Bake for a final 25 minutes, or until the vegetables are very tender and the haloumi is golden and heated through.

Meanwhile, make the tomato sauce. In a saucepan, heat the olive oil over medium–high heat. Add the onion and cook, stirring, for 8 minutes, or until softened. Add the garlic and cook for a further 2 minutes. Add the tomatoes and thyme and simmer for 20 minutes, or until the sauce has reduced by half. Season to taste with sea salt and freshly ground black pepper.

Serve the vegetables topped with the tomato sauce and sprinkled with the parsley. Accompany with the yoghurt.

Haloumi is a salty, semi-firm cheese made from sheep's milk. It has a rubbery texture, but becomes soft and deliciously chewy when fried or baked and served warm.
Turlu turlu is a Turkish dish of slow-cooked vegetables, similar to a baked ratatouille but with a spicy kick. This is a baked version of this dish. Serve with toasted Turkish bread if desired.

Pad see hew

This vegetarian version of the Thai rice noodle dish uses tempeh in place of meat. Like tofu, tempeh is made from split soya beans, but has a deep, nutty flavour and more protein, fibre and vitamins than tofu.

Sambal oelek is a hot paste made from crushed fresh red chillies, mixed with salt and vinegar.

Fresh rice noodles can be thick or thin, or sold in a sheet that can be cut to the desired width. To loosen and separate the noodles, simply rinse them in hot water, then drain. They are added to stir-fries or simmered dishes near the end of cooking as they only need to be heated through. You'll find all these ingredients in Asian grocery stores and large supermarkets.

80 ml (2½ fl oz/⅓ cup) kecap manis
2 tablespoons light soy sauce
1 tablespoon sambal oelek
1 tablespoon sugar
60 ml (2 fl oz/¼ cup) peanut oil
3 eggs, lightly beaten
100 g (3½ oz) tempeh, cut into thin
   strips, approximately 5 mm x 3 cm
   (¼ x 1¼ inches)
3 garlic cloves, finely chopped
2 bunches (about 750 g/1 lb 10 oz each)
   Chinese broccoli (gai larn), tough stem
   ends discarded, leaves coarsely shredded
450 g (1 lb) fresh flat rice
   noodles, separated
1–2 red bird's eye chillies, thinly sliced on
   the diagonal
50 g (1¾ oz/⅓ cup) roasted peanuts,
   coarsely chopped
lime wedges, to serve

In a small bowl, mix together the kecap manis, soy sauce, sambal oelek and sugar. Set aside.

In a large wok, heat 1 tablespoon of the oil over high heat and swirl to coat the side. Add the eggs and cook for about 1 minute, pushing the outside cooked areas into the centre as they cook. When the egg has set, transfer the omelette to a cutting board and cut into 1 cm (½ inch)-wide strips. Set aside.

Heat the remaining oil in the wok. Add the tempeh and stir-fry for 2–3 minutes, or until just golden. Remove with a slotted spoon and drain on paper towels.

Stir-fry the garlic in the wok for 30 seconds. Add the broccoli and cook, tossing the wok, for 2–3 minutes. Add the noodles and kecap manis mixture and stir-fry for a further 2–3 minutes. Add the tempeh and omelette strips and toss to combine and heat through.

Divide the noodle mixture among serving bowls. Sprinkle with the chilli and peanuts and serve with lime wedges.

Preparation time: 20 minutes · Cooking time: 15 minutes · Serves: 4

Preparation time: 35 minutes
plus 20 minutes cooling

Cooking time:
2 hours 10 minutes

Serves: 4

Caramelised onion tarte tatin

4 large brown onions (about 250 g/
  9 oz each)
2 tablespoons olive oil
1½ tablespoons rosemary
20 g (¾ oz) butter, diced
1½ tablespoons good-quality
  balsamic vinegar
1 sheet frozen puff pastry, thawed
  and chilled

**Watercress, walnut and goat's
  cheese salad**
2 handfuls picked watercress sprigs
60 g (2¼ oz/½ cup) coarsely
  chopped walnuts
1 tablespoon balsamic vinegar
50 ml (1½ fl oz) extra virgin olive oil
100 g (3½ oz) soft goat's cheese,
  coarsely crumbled

Preheat the oven to 150°C (300°F/Gas 2). Line a large baking tray with baking paper.

Keeping the skin on, remove a thin slice from the top and root ends of the onions. Slice the onions into 1.5 cm (⅝ inch)-thick rounds and place on the baking tray in a single layer. In a bowl, mix together the olive oil and 1 tablespoon rosemary and season with sea salt and freshly ground black pepper. Brush the mixture over the onion rounds and bake for 1½–1¾ hours, or until the onion is well caramelised and softened, turning the slices over halfway during cooking. Remove from the oven and allow to cool for 20 minutes.

Increase the oven temperature to 220°C (425°F/Gas 7). Peel the outside skin and any tough pieces from the onion. Place one onion round in the middle of an 18 cm (7 inch) heavy-based ovenproof frying pan, then arrange more onion rounds tightly around it. Season to taste. Repeat with another layer of onion and season to taste. Scatter the butter over the onion and drizzle with the vinegar.

Cut a 22 cm (8½ inch) circle from the pastry, then place it over the onion, tucking it well down the side of the pan around the onion. Bake for 22–25 minutes, or until the pastry is golden brown and crisp.

Near serving time, prepare the salad. Place the watercress and walnuts in a bowl. Combine the vinegar and olive oil and season to taste. Pour over the salad and gently toss. Sprinkle with the goat's cheese.

Remove the tart from the oven and loosen the edges with a spatula. Place a plate or cutting board on top of the frying pan, then carefully invert the tart onto the plate, onion side up. Scatter the remaining rosemary over the tart.

Cut the tart into quarters and place on serving plates. Serve with the salad.

Spiced sweet potato coils
with couscous salad

When using preserved lemon, scrape off and discard the inner flesh, which is bitter and very salty. The skin is valued for the intense lemon tang it adds to dishes. It too is quite salty, so you can reduce the amount of salt you season the final dish with. Preserved lemon quarters are available from larger supermarkets, fine food stores and delicatessens. If you don't have any, you can use grated lemon rind, but the flavour won't be quite the same.

It is best to use chilled filo pastry from the refrigerated section of the supermarket rather than thawed frozen filo pastry as it is easier to work with and shape and doesn't become brittle.

2 orange sweet potatoes (about 1 kg/
  2 lb 4 oz), peeled and cut into 2 cm
  (¾ inch) chunks
3 garlic cloves, crushed
1 onion, chopped
2 teaspoons ground cumin
1 teaspoon ground coriander
½ teaspoon ground cinnamon
2 tablespoons olive oil
60 ml (2 fl oz/¼ cup) orange juice
100 g (3½ oz/¾ cup) walnuts, chopped
2 tablespoons coriander (cilantro)
  leaves, chopped
375 g (13 oz) packet filo pastry sheets
100 g (3½ oz) butter, melted
1 tablespoon sesame seeds
1 tablespoon poppy seeds

Couscous salad
95 g (3¼ oz/½ cup) instant couscous
2 tablespoons olive oil
1 tablespoon lemon juice
1 small handful flat-leaf (Italian) parsley,
  chopped
1 small handful mint, chopped
6 dried dates, finely chopped
2 teaspoons chopped preserved lemon,
  or to taste

Preheat the oven to 180°C (350°F/Gas 4).

Place the sweet potato in a bowl with the garlic, onion, spices and olive oil. Season to taste with sea salt and freshly ground black pepper and mix well to coat the sweet potato. Transfer to a baking dish and bake for 30 minutes, or until the sweet potato is cooked through. Place in a bowl and leave to cool.

Lightly mash the cooled sweet potato using a potato masher or fork. Mix in the orange juice, walnuts and coriander and season to taste.

Increase the oven temperature to 200°C (400°F/Gas 6). Place the filo pastry on a tray and cover with a damp tea towel (dish towel).

Line a 35 x 27 cm (14 x 10¾ inch) baking tray with baking paper. Place one pastry sheet on a clean work surface and brush lightly with melted butter. Top with another sheet of pastry. Place one-quarter of the sweet potato mixture in a long strip 1 cm (½ inch) wide along one edge of the pastry. Gently roll up the pastry to make a cylinder, enclosing the filling — don't roll too tightly or the pastry might split. Now gently coil the cylinder into a scroll shape, then place on the baking tray and brush with butter to stop it drying out. Repeat with the remaining pastry, filling and butter to make four coils in total.

Sprinkle the coils with the sesame and poppy seeds, then bake for 30 minutes, or until the pastry is crisp and golden.

When the coils are nearly ready, place the couscous in a bowl, stir in 125 ml (4 fl oz/½ cup) warm water and 1 tablespoon of the olive oil, then cover and leave to stand for 5 minutes. Fluff the grains up with a fork, then stir in the remaining olive oil and remaining salad ingredients. Season to taste.

Serve the sweet potato coils hot, with the couscous salad.

Preparation time: 40 minutes Cooking time: 1 hour Serves: 4

Vegetable skewers with parsnip skordalia

2 red capsicums (peppers), cut into
  2 cm (¾ inch) pieces
3 Japanese eggplants (aubergines),
  cut into 1 cm (½ inch)-thick rounds
3 zucchini (courgettes), cut into 1 cm
  (½ inch)-thick rounds
2 tablespoons olive oil
½ teaspoon dried oregano
350 g (12 oz) haloumi cheese,
  cut into 2 cm (¾ inch) cubes
chopped flat-leaf (Italian) parsley,
  to garnish
lemon wedges, to serve

Parsnip skordalia

500 g (1 lb 2 oz) parsnips, peeled, core
  removed and chopped
300 g (10½ oz) sebago or other floury
  potatoes, peeled and chopped
60 ml (2 fl oz/¼ cup) olive oil
2 tablespoons lemon juice
3–4 garlic cloves, crushed

Soak 12 bamboo skewers in cold water for
30 minutes to prevent scorching.

To make the parsnip skordalia, place the
parsnip and potato in a saucepan of boiling water
and cook for 15–20 minutes, or until very tender.
Drain well, then mash until smooth. (Do not use a
food processor to mash the mixture or the potato
will become gluey.) Transfer the mixture to a bowl
and stir in the olive oil, lemon juice and garlic
until well combined. Cover to keep warm.

Meanwhile, preheat the grill (broiler) to
medium–high. Place the capsicum, eggplant and
zucchini in a bowl. Add the olive oil and oregano
and toss to coat the vegetables.

Thread the vegetables and haloumi
alternately onto the skewers. Grill the skewers,
turning regularly, for 10–12 minutes, or until
the vegetables are tender and the haloumi
is lightly golden.

Divide the warm skordalia among serving
plates or shallow bowls. Top with the skewers.
Garnish with parsley and serve immediately, with
lemon wedges.

Traditionally served with fried fish
or vegetables, skordalia is a thick,
garlicky Greek sauce or dip based
on puréed potatoes. Here parsnip
adds a subtle sweetness, but to
vary the recipe you could also
use cooked white beans such as
cannellini. Turkish bread makes
a lovely accompaniment to round
out the meal.

Carrot and almond gougère

A speciality of the French region of Burgundy, a gougère is a savoury choux pastry flavoured with cheese — sometimes comté or emmental, but usually gruyère, a firm cow's milk cheese with a smooth texture and natural rind. Gruyère has a nutty flavour and melts easily, making it perfect for tarts, gratins and dishes such as this.

75 g (2½ oz) butter, chopped
1 teaspoon sea salt
110 g (3¾ oz/¾ cup) plain
   (all-purpose) flour
3 eggs
35 g (1¼ oz/¼ cup) finely grated
   gruyère cheese
1 teaspoon mustard powder
salad leaves, to serve
25 g (1 oz/¼ cup) toasted flaked almonds
2 tablespoons chervil

Carrot filling
50 g (1¾ oz) butter
1 small brown onion, finely chopped
1 garlic clove, crushed
¼ teaspoon cayenne pepper
2 carrots, coarsely grated
1 small handful flat-leaf (Italian) parsley,
   finely chopped
1½ tablespoons plain (all-purpose) flour
500 ml (17 fl oz/2 cups) milk
50 g (1¾ oz/⅓ cup) finely grated
   gruyère cheese

Preheat the oven to 200°C (400°F/Gas 6). Line two baking trays with baking paper.

Place the butter, salt and 185 ml (6 fl oz/ ¾ cup) water in a small saucepan over medium heat. Cook, without allowing to boil, for 3 minutes, or until the butter has melted. Add the flour all at once and stir vigorously for 1–2 minutes, or until the mixture forms a ball that comes away from the side of the pan.

Transfer the mixture to the small bowl of an electric mixer. Add the eggs, one at a time, beating well after each addition until combined. Beat in the gruyère and mustard powder.

Spoon the mixture into a piping (icing) bag fitted with a 1 cm (½ inch) plain nozzle, then pipe six 8 cm (3¼ inch) rounds on the baking trays. Bake for 20 minutes.

Reduce the oven temperature to 180°C (350°F/Gas 4) and bake for a further 10 minutes, or until the gougères are a deep golden brown. Remove from the oven, allow to cool slightly.

Meanwhile, make the carrot filling. Melt 20 g (¾ oz) of the butter in a frying pan over medium heat. Add the onion and cook, stirring, for 8 minutes, or until softened. Add the garlic and cayenne pepper and cook for 1 minute. Add the carrot and cook, stirring occasionally, for 10 minutes, or until the carrot has softened. Transfer to a bowl. Stir in the parsley.

Melt the remaining butter in a saucepan over medium heat. Add the flour and cook, stirring, for 2 minutes, or until the mixture bubbles and thickens. Remove from the heat and gradually whisk in the milk. Bring to the boil over medium heat, reduce heat to low and simmer, stirring, for 3 minutes. Stir in the gruyère and season to taste with sea salt and freshly ground black pepper. Stir the sauce into the carrot mixture.

Place some salad leaves on each serving plate and top with the bottom halves of the gougères. Fill with the carrot mixture and sprinkle with the almonds and chervil. Top with the lids and serve.

Preparation time: 20 minutes **Cooking time:** 35 minutes **Serves:** 6

Preparation time: 15 minutes   **Cooking time:** 25 minutes   **Serves:** 4

Five-spice braised eggplant with tofu and bok choy

60 ml (2 fl oz/¼ cup) peanut oil

750 g (1 lb 10 oz) Japanese eggplants (aubergines), sliced diagonally into 3 cm (1¼ inch) lengths

2 garlic cloves, crushed

½ teaspoon Chinese five-spice powder

125 ml (4 fl oz/½ cup) dry sherry

125 ml (4 fl oz/½ cup) vegetable stock

1 tablespoon char siu sauce

1 tablespoon orange juice

300 g (10½ oz) firm tofu, drained and cut into small cubes

½ teaspoon sesame oil

3 bok choy (pak choy), about 400 g (14 oz), halved lengthways, then sliced

1 small handful coriander (cilantro) leaves

1 long red chilli, thinly sliced

2 teaspoons toasted sesame seeds

steamed rice, to serve

Heat 2 tablespoons of the peanut oil in a large wok or frying pan over high heat. Add the eggplant and cook, stirring, for 5 minutes, or until lightly browned. Remove from the wok.

Heat the remaining peanut oil in the wok. Add the garlic and five-spice and cook, stirring, for 1 minute, or until aromatic. Add the sherry and bring to the boil. Reduce the heat to low and simmer, uncovered, for 2 minutes, or until the liquid has reduced by half.

Add the stock, char siu sauce and orange juice and bring back to the boil. Reduce the heat to low, return the eggplant to the wok and simmer, uncovered, for 10 minutes. Add the tofu and simmer for 2 minutes, or until warmed through. Stir in the sesame oil.

Meanwhile, bring 1.5 cm (⅝ inch) water to the boil in a large saucepan. Add the bok choy, cover tightly and steam for 2 minutes, or until the leaves have wilted and the stems have softened. Drain well.

Divide the bok choy and eggplant braise among serving bowls and sprinkle with the coriander, chilli and sesame seeds. Serve with steamed rice.

Also known as Chinese barbecue sauce, char siu sauce adds a sweet, smoky flavour to marinades, braises and stir-fries. You'll find it in Asian grocery stores and large supermarkets.

Silverbeet, rice and parmesan tart

For this recipe start with an untrimmed bunch of silverbeet weighing about 1 kg (2 lb 4 oz). After cutting off the thick white stems you'll be left with about 250 g (9 oz) of leaves.

1 tablespoon olive oil
1 brown onion, finely chopped
1 garlic clove, crushed
½ teaspoon freshly ground nutmeg
250 g (9 oz) silverbeet (Swiss chard) leaves, shredded
110 g (3¾ oz/½ cup) short-grain white rice
250 ml (9 fl oz/1 cup) milk
300 ml (10½ fl oz) pouring cream
2 egg yolks
75 g (2½ oz/¾ cup) grated parmesan cheese
50 g (1¾ oz/⅓ cup) pine nuts
rocket (arugula), avocado and cherry tomato salad, to serve

Pastry

250 g (9 oz/1⅔ cups) plain (all-purpose) flour
2 teaspoons finely grated lemon rind
125 g (4½ oz) unsalted butter, chopped
1 egg yolk, lightly beaten with 2 teaspoons water

To make the pastry, sift the flour into a large bowl, add the lemon rind, then rub in the butter until the mixture resembles coarse breadcrumbs. Add the egg yolk mixture and mix until a dough forms. Turn out onto a lightly floured surface and roll the pastry to a circle large enough to line a 22 cm (8½ inch) fluted, loose-based flan (tart) tin. Ease the pastry into the tin, then trim the edges. Cover and refrigerate for 30 minutes.

Preheat the oven to 180°C (350°F/Gas 4). Place the flan tin on a baking tray. Line the pastry shell with baking paper, then fill with baking beads, dried beans or rice. Bake for 15 minutes, then remove the beads or rice and paper. Bake for a further 5 minutes, or until the pastry is lightly golden.

Meanwhile, heat the olive oil in a large frying pan over medium heat. Add the onion and cook, stirring, for 8 minutes, or until softened. Add the garlic and nutmeg and cook for 1 minute. Add the silverbeet, then cover and cook over low heat, stirring occasionally, for 5 minutes, or until the silverbeet is tender. Transfer the mixture to a large bowl.

In a saucepan, combine the rice, milk and 125 ml (4 fl oz/½ cup) of the cream. Stir over medium heat until the mixture comes to the boil. Reduce the heat to low, then cover and cook for 10 minutes, stirring occasionally. Remove from the heat, then stir in the egg yolks, parmesan and remaining cream.

Stir the rice mixture into the silverbeet mixture, then spoon into the pastry case. Sprinkle with the pine nuts and bake for 20 minutes, or until the filling has set. Remove from the oven and leave to stand for 10 minutes.

Cut the tart into wedges and serve with the rocket, avocado and cherry tomato salad.

Preparation time: 25 minutes   Cooking time: 25 minutes   Serves: 4

Mee rebus

450 g (1 lb) sweet potato, peeled and
cut into 2 cm (¾ inch) cubes
4 eggs
2 teaspoons finely grated palm
sugar (jaggery)
60 ml (2 fl oz/¼ cup) yellow bean sauce
2 tablespoons light soy sauce
800 ml (28 fl oz) vegetable stock
500 g (1 lb 2 oz) fresh hokkien
(egg) noodles
1 Lebanese (short) cucumber, cut into
long matchsticks
2 spring onions (scallions), cut into
long, thin strips
3 tofu puffs, cut into 5 mm
(¼ inch)-thick slices
2 bird's eye chillies, thinly sliced
30 g (1 oz/¼ cup) fried Asian shallots,
to serve (optional)
lime wedges, to serve

Spice paste
6 macadamia nuts, toasted
6 red Asian shallots, chopped
1 tablespoon chopped fresh ginger
3 garlic cloves, chopped
2 teaspoons finely grated fresh
galangal (optional)
2 lemongrass stems, white part only,
thinly sliced
2 teaspoons freshly ground
white peppercorns
80 ml (2½ fl oz/⅓ cup) peanut oil
1 tablespoon Malaysian curry powder

Place the sweet potato in a steamer or bamboo basket set over a saucepan of boiling water. Cover and cook for 10–12 minutes, or until tender. Transfer to a bowl and mash.

Meanwhile, to make the spice paste, place the macadamias in a food processor with the shallot, ginger, garlic, galangal, lemongrass and pepper. Pulse until finely chopped. Add the oil and curry powder and blend until a smooth paste forms.

Bring a small saucepan of water to a simmer. Gently lower the eggs in and cook for 6 minutes. Drain the eggs and cool slightly under cold water. Peel and set aside.

Heat a wok over medium heat. Add the spice paste and cook over medium heat, stirring constantly, for 5 minutes, or until aromatic. Add the palm sugar, yellow bean sauce, soy sauce, stock and mashed sweet potato, stirring well. Increase the heat to high and stir until all the ingredients are heated through. Season to taste with sea salt and freshly ground black pepper.

Meanwhile, place the noodles in a heatproof bowl and cover with boiling water. Leave to stand for 2 minutes, or until softened. Drain well.

Divide the noodles among serving bowls and pour the spice mixture over. Halve the eggs, then place on the noodles with the cucumber, spring onion, tofu, chilli and fried shallots, if desired. Serve with lime wedges.

Mee rebus is a spicy noodle dish popular in Indonesia, Singapore and Malaysia.

Yellow bean sauce is made from fermented soya beans and is sold in Asian grocery stores; hoisin sauce may be used as a substitute.

Fried Asian shallots are very thin slices of red Asian shallots that have been deep-fried until crisp. They are used as a crunchy, flavoursome garnish and are sold in packets in Asian grocery stores.

To toast the macadamias, place them on a small baking tray and bake in a preheated 180°C (350°F/ Gas 4) oven for 10 minutes, or until lightly golden.

Related to ginger, galangal is a pink-coloured root that looks similar to ginger, but has a distinctive peppery flavour. Like ginger it should be peeled before using.

Salt and pepper tofu with snow peas

A handful of coriander (cilantro) leaves can also be scattered over the tofu before serving.

2 teaspoons freshly ground sichuan peppercorns
1 teaspoon freshly ground white pepper
2 tablespoons sea salt
75 g (2½ oz/½ cup) plain (all-purpose) flour
600 g (1 lb 5 oz) firm silken tofu, drained and cut into 8 squares
350 g (12 oz) snow peas (mangetout), trimmed
1 litre (35 fl oz/4 cups) vegetable oil
5 garlic cloves, thinly sliced
2 long red chillies, thinly sliced on the diagonal
8 red Asian shallots, thinly sliced on the diagonal
steamed rice, to serve
lemon wedges, to serve
soy sauce, to serve

Place the peppercorns, salt and flour in a bowl and mix well. Working in batches, gently coat the tofu with the flour mixture, shaking off the excess. Set aside.

Bring a saucepan of lightly salted water to the boil over medium–high heat. Blanch the snow peas for 30 seconds, drain, then transfer to a plate and keep warm.

Heat the oil in a saucepan over medium–high heat to 180°C (350°F). The oil is ready when a cube of bread dropped into the oil turns golden in 15 seconds.

Add half the tofu to the oil and deep-fry for 1–2 minutes, or until golden and crisp. Remove with a slotted spoon and drain on paper towels. Repeat with the remaining tofu.

Add the garlic, chilli and shallot to the oil and cook for 1 minute. Remove using a slotted spoon and drain on paper towels.

Divide the steamed rice among serving bowls. Top with the tofu and snow peas, then garnish with the fried garlic, chilli and shallot. Serve with lemon wedges and soy sauce.

Preparation time: 25 minutes **Cooking time:** 15 minutes **Serves:** 4

Preparation time: 30 minutes
plus 1 hour chilling

Cooking time:
1 hour 20 minutes

Serves: 4–6

Vegetarian 'meatballs' in
North African-spiced tomato sauce

185 ml (6 fl oz/¾ cup) olive oil

2 brown onions, finely chopped

5 garlic cloves, crushed

50 g (1¾ oz/⅓ cup) currants

1 tablespoon cumin seeds, lightly toasted and coarsely crushed

500 g (1 lb 2 oz/6¼ cups) fresh breadcrumbs, made from day-old bread

200 g (7 oz/1⅓ cups) crumbled feta cheese

2 large handfuls mint leaves, chopped, plus extra, to garnish

2 large handfuls flat-leaf (Italian) parsley, chopped, plus extra, to garnish

4 eggs, lightly beaten

North African-spiced tomato sauce

2 tablespoons olive oil

2 brown onions, finely chopped

1½ teaspoons paprika

½ teaspoon chilli powder, or to taste

½ teaspoon ground ginger

3 x 400 g (14 oz) tins chopped tomatoes

1 tablespoon finely chopped preserved lemon rind, or to taste, plus extra thin slices, to garnish

1 handful coriander (cilantro) leaves, finely chopped

Heat 2 tablespoons of the olive oil in a non-stick frying pan over medium heat. Add the onion and cook, stirring, for 8 minutes, or until softened. Add the garlic, currants and cumin and cook for 1 minute.

Line a baking tray with baking paper. Transfer the onion mixture to a large bowl and add the breadcrumbs, feta, mint, parsley and eggs. Season with sea salt and freshly ground black pepper, then mix well with your hands, adding a little milk if needed to bind the mixture together — the mixture should be firm and not sticky. Working with 2 tablespoons of the mixture at a time, form the mixture into balls. Place on the baking tray and refrigerate for 1 hour, or until firm.

Meanwhile, make the North African-spiced tomato sauce. Heat the olive oil in a saucepan over medium heat. Add the onion and cook, stirring, for 8 minutes, or until softened. Add the spices and cook, stirring, for a further 1 minute, or until aromatic. Add the tomato and bring to the boil, then reduce the heat to low and simmer for 35–40 minutes, stirring occasionally, or until rich and thick. Stir in the preserved lemon and coriander and season to taste. Keep warm.

Heat half the remaining oil in a frying pan over medium–high heat. Cook half the balls for 5–7 minutes, rolling them around in the pan to brown on all sides. Remove and drain on paper towels. Heat the remaining oil in the pan, cook the remaining balls.

Divide the sauce among serving bowls. Top with the balls, garnish with the extra mint, parsley and preserved lemon, and serve.

To lightly toast the cumin seeds, put them in a small frying pan without any oil and cook for a few minutes over medium heat, or until aromatic, shaking the pan and keeping an eye on the seeds to ensure they don't burn. Crush them in a mortar using a pestle. This dish is not suitable for freezing.

Tofu steak with fried eggplant, daikon and red miso dressing

As an alternative the tofu could be cut into 2 cm (¾ inch) cubes, prepared as directed, then tossed with the dressing and other ingredients.

Dashi powder, red miso paste, tamari and mirin are used in Japanese cuisine and are sold in Asian grocery stores and larger supermarkets.

Also popular in Japanese cooking, daikon is a large, white, carrot-shaped radish with a mild, slightly peppery flavour. Choose firm, shiny daikon with unscarred skin and peel before using. It is also available from Asian grocery stores and larger supermarkets.

2 small eggplants (aubergines), about 700 g (1 lb 9 oz), each cut into 8 wedges
250 ml (9 fl oz/1 cup) vegetable oil
rice flour, for dusting
freshly ground white pepper, for seasoning
600 g (1 lb 5 oz) firm tofu, drained and cut into 1 cm (½ inch)-thick slices
90 g (3¼ oz/1 cup) finely grated daikon
mixed baby salad greens, to serve

Red miso dressing
2 teaspoons instant dashi powder
1 tablespoon red miso paste
1 tablespoon tamari
1½ tablespoons mirin
1 teaspoon sugar

Place the eggplant in a colander and sprinkle with sea salt. Leave to stand for 30 minutes, then rinse well and pat dry using paper towels.

Preheat the oven to 120°C (235°F/Gas ½). Heat 80 ml (2½ fl oz/⅓ cup) of the oil in a non-stick frying pan over medium–high heat. Add half the eggplant and cook for 2 minutes on each side, or until golden. Remove and drain on paper towels on a baking tray. Fry the remaining eggplant, adding more oil to the pan as necessary. Drain on paper towels, then transfer the baking tray to the oven to keep warm.

Season some rice flour with freshly ground white pepper. Pat the tofu slices dry with paper towels, then lightly coat in the rice flour, dusting off the excess. Heat the remaining oil in the frying pan over medium–high heat. Cook the tofu for 1–2 minutes on each side, or until golden. Remove and drain on paper towels.

Meanwhile, make the red miso dressing. Bring 200 ml (7 fl oz) water to a simmer in a saucepan. Add the dressing ingredients and stir to dissolve the sugar — do not allow to boil.

Divide the tofu among shallow serving bowls. Top with the eggplant wedges and spoon the dressing over. Scatter with the daikon, garnish with salad greens and serve.

Preparation time: 10 minutes
plus 30 minutes standing

Cooking time: 20 minutes

Serves: 4

Mushroom, dill and cream cheese coulibiac

100 g (3½ oz/½ cup) long-grain rice
20 g (¾ oz) butter
1 tablespoon olive oil
500 g (1 lb 2 oz) mushrooms caps,
  wiped clean and finely chopped
2 garlic cloves, crushed
1 tablespoon snipped chives
250 g (9 oz/1 cup) cream
  cheese, softened
¼ cup finely chopped dill
1 tablespoon drained small capers
2 teaspoons lemon juice
4 sheets frozen puff pastry,
  partially thawed
1 egg, whisked with 1 tablespoon milk
mixed salad leaves, to serve
tomato relish, to serve

Bring 250 ml (9 fl oz/1 cup) water to the boil in a saucepan over medium–high heat. Add the rice, stir briefly and return to the boil. Cover, reduce the heat to low and cook for 10 minutes, or until the rice is tender and the water is absorbed. Remove from the heat and allow to stand for 10 minutes.

Meanwhile, heat the butter and olive oil in a large non-stick frying pan. Add the mushrooms and garlic and cook, stirring, for 4–5 minutes, or until the mushrooms are tender. Remove from the heat and season with sea salt and freshly ground black pepper. Stir in the chives, then set aside to cool.

In a bowl, beat together the cream cheese, dill, capers and lemon juice. Season to taste and set aside.

Preheat the oven to 220°C (425°F/Gas 7). Line two large baking trays with baking paper.

Cut each pastry sheet in half. Place four pastry pieces on the baking trays. Divide the rice among the pieces, spreading it evenly and leaving a 3 cm (1¼ inch) border. Spoon the mushroom mixture over the rice, then dot the cream cheese mixture over the mushrooms.

Lightly brush the pastry borders with some of the beaten egg. Place the remaining pastry pieces over each mound to cover, then press the edges together with a fork to seal. Cut three slits in each pastry top to allow the steam to escape, then brush with more egg mixture.

Bake for 20–25 minutes, or until the pastry is puffed, golden and cooked through.

Remove from the oven and allow to stand for 10 minutes before slicing. Serve with mixed salad leaves and tomato relish.

Originally a Russian dish known as kulebiaka, but adopted by the French as their own, coulibiac traditionally is a type of salmon, rice and mushroom pie, encased in brioche dough or puff pastry. Ensure the rice and mushrooms are thoroughly cooled before filling the coulibiac or the pastry will be soggy.

Spicy chickpea pot pie

To save time, instead of soaking and cooking dried chickpeas, you can use two 400 g (14 oz) tins of chickpeas in the pie. Rinse and drain them well before using.

220 g (7¾ oz/1 cup) dried chickpeas
60 ml (2 fl oz/¼ cup) olive oil
1 brown onion, finely chopped
400 g (14 oz) tin chopped tomatoes
60 g (2¼ oz/¼ cup) tomato paste
  (concentrated purée)
¼ teaspoon ground cardamom
2 tablespoons pomegranate molasses
1 garlic clove, crushed
1 bunch (about 250 g/9 oz) English
  spinach, tough stems removed, leaves
  washed and drained
1 tablespoon chopped mint leaves
2 tablespoons chopped coriander
  (cilantro) leaves

Potato mash
6 Dutch cream or other waxy potatoes
  (about 700 g/1 lb 9 oz in total), peeled
  and coarsely chopped
1 garlic clove, crushed
60 ml (2 fl oz/¼ cup) extra virgin olive oil
125 ml (4 fl oz/½ cup) milk
1 tablespoon chopped flat-leaf
  (Italian) parsley
125 g (4½ oz/¾ cup) feta cheese,
  crumbled

Place the chickpeas in a bowl. Cover with cold water and leave to soak overnight.

Drain the chickpeas and place in a saucepan. Add enough water to cover by 3 cm (1¼ inches). Bring to the boil over high heat, then reduce the heat and simmer for 1 hour, or until the chickpeas are tender. Drain and set aside.

Meanwhile, make the potato mash. Place the potato in a saucepan and cover with water. Bring to the boil over high heat and cook for 20 minutes, or until very tender. Drain well, then return to the saucepan. Add the garlic, olive oil, milk and parsley and mash, using a potato masher, until smooth. Stir in the feta and season to taste with sea salt and freshly ground black pepper.

Preheat the oven to 180°C (350°F/Gas 4).

Heat the oil in a heavy-based saucepan over medium heat. Add the onion and cook, stirring occasionally, for 8 minutes, or until softened. Add the tomato, tomato paste, cardamom, pomegranate molasses, garlic and 125 ml (4 fl oz/½ cup) water. Cook for 10 minutes, stirring occasionally. Stir in the chickpeas and spinach and cook for 2–3 minutes, or until the spinach has wilted. Season to taste, then stir in the mint and coriander.

Spoon the chickpea mixture into a 1.5 litre (52 fl oz/6 cup) baking dish, or divide among four 400 ml (14 fl oz) individual ovenproof dishes. Spoon the mashed potato over the top to cover.

Bake for 20 minutes, or until the potato topping is lightly golden. Serve hot.

Preparation time: 30 minutes
plus overnight soaking

Cooking time:
1 hour 45 minutes

Serves: 4

Preparation time: 25 minutes
plus overnight soaking and 1 hour chilling

Cooking time: 2 hours
10 minutes

Serves: 6–8

Georgian bean pie

280 g (10 oz/1⅓ cups) dried kidney
  beans, soaked overnight and drained
30 g (1 oz) butter
2 brown onions, finely chopped
2 teaspoons ground coriander
225 g (8 oz/1½ cups) grated
  mozzarella cheese
150 g (5½ oz/1 cup) crumbled feta
  cheese
1 large handful flat-leaf (Italian)
  parsley, chopped
1 large handful coriander (cilantro)
  leaves, chopped
mixed salad leaves, to serve

Walnut shortcrust pastry

300 g (10½ oz/2 cups) plain
  (all-purpose) flour
150 g (5½ oz/1 cup) wholemeal
  (whole-wheat) flour
1 teaspoon bicarbonate of soda
  (baking soda)
60 g (2¼ oz/½ cup) finely
  chopped walnuts
200 g (7 oz) sour cream
125 g (4½ oz) butter, melted and cooled
3 egg yolks

To make the walnut shortcrust pastry, sift the flours and bicarbonate of soda into a large bowl, returning any wholemeal flour solids to the bowl. Stir in the walnuts. In another bowl mix together the sour cream, butter and 2 egg yolks until combined, then add to the flour mixture. Using a flat-bladed knife, stir until a dough forms, adding a little iced water if the mixture is too dry. Turn out onto a floured surface and knead briefly until smooth. Form into a disc, wrap in plastic wrap and refrigerate for 1 hour.

Meanwhile, place the beans in a saucepan of water and bring to the boil. Reduce the heat and simmer for 1 hour, or until very tender, skimming off any froth. Drain well, then place in a bowl.

Melt the butter in a frying pan over medium heat. Add the onion and cook, stirring, for 8 minutes, or until softened. Add to the beans and crush lightly using a potato masher. Stir in the ground coriander, cheeses and herbs until well combined. Season to taste with sea salt and freshly ground black pepper. Set aside to cool.

Preheat the oven to 180°C (350°F/Gas 4). Lightly grease and flour the side of a 24 cm (9½ inch) springform cake tin, then line the base with baking paper. On a lightly floured surface, roll two-thirds of the chilled pastry out into a circle large enough to cover the base and side of the tin, then ease the pastry into the tin. Whisk the remaining egg yolk with 2 teaspoons water and lightly brush around the pastry edge. Spoon the bean filling into the pastry shell, packing it in evenly.

Roll the remaining pastry out into a circle large enough to cover the pie, then place over the filling. Trim the pastry edges, then press or crimp to seal well. Brush the top with more egg yolk, then cut a cross in the middle of the top using a small sharp knife to allow the steam to escape.

Bake for 1 hour, or until the pastry is cooked through and golden. Serve warm or at room temperature, with mixed salad leaves.

Thai pineapple and tofu fried rice

When making fried rice dishes, you'll get the best results if you cook the rice the day before and refrigerate it overnight. It's a great way of using up leftover rice.

1 small ripe pineapple
1 tablespoon peanut oil
150 g (5½ oz) snake (yard long) beans, cut into 5 cm (2 inch) lengths
4 red Asian shallots, finely chopped
4 garlic cloves, finely chopped
2 teaspoons grated fresh ginger
300 g (10½ oz/1½ cups) long-grain white rice, cooked
125 ml (4 fl oz/½ cup) vegetable stock
1 small carrot, coarsely grated
4 tofu puffs, cut into 1 cm (½ inch) cubes
3 spring onions (scallions), thinly sliced on the diagonal
2 tablespoons soy sauce
50 g (1¾ oz/⅓ cup) chopped roasted cashew nuts
1 small handful coriander (cilantro) leaves
2 long red chillies, seeded and thinly sliced

Cut the skin off the pineapple and remove any eyes. Remove the core, then cut the pineapple into 1 cm (½ inch) cubes. Set aside.

Heat the oil in a wok or frying pan over medium–high heat, swirling to coat the side. Add the snake beans and cook for 1–2 minutes, then add the shallot, garlic and ginger and stir-fry for 1 minute.

Add the cooked rice and stock and stir-fry for 3 minutes, or until the rice is heated through. Add the pineapple, carrot, tofu and spring onion and stir-fry for 3 minutes. Add the soy sauce and toss to combine.

Divide the fried rice among serving bowls and serve sprinkled with the cashews, coriander and chilli.

Preparation time: 25 minutes   **Cooking time:** 10 minutes   **Serves:** 4

Preparation time: 45 minutes

Cooking time: 1 hour 20 minutes

Serves: 4–6

Tunisian vegetable stew with lemon pickle

2 tablespoons olive oil
1 large brown onion, finely sliced
3 garlic cloves, finely chopped
2 teaspoons ground coriander
1 teaspoon ground turmeric
½ teaspoon ground cinnamon
1–2 tablespoons tomato paste
(concentrated purée)
750 ml (26 fl oz/3 cups) vegetable stock
2 potatoes (about 400 g/14 oz), peeled
and cut into 2 cm (¾ inch) chunks
100 g (3½ oz/1⅓ cups) thinly
sliced cabbage
150 g (5½ oz/1 cup) fresh pitted
dates, chopped
150 g (5½ oz/1¼ cups) small
cauliflower florets
200 g (7 oz) green beans, trimmed and
halved diagonally
steamed couscous, to serve
1 large handful coriander (cilantro)
leaves, chopped, to serve (optional)
35 g (1¼ oz/¼ cup) chopped pistachio
nuts, to serve (optional)

Lemon pickle
3 lemons (about 450g/1 lb)
1 tablespoon olive oil
1 brown onion, thinly sliced
1 tablespoon finely grated fresh ginger
2 garlic cloves, crushed
1 teaspoon yellow mustard seeds
½ teaspoon ground allspice
1 teaspoon ground coriander
½ teaspoon hot chilli powder
200 ml (7 fl oz) cider vinegar
1½ teaspoons sea salt
55 g (2 oz/¼ cup) sugar

To make the lemon pickle, cut the lemons in half widthways, juice the lemons, then strain the juice and set aside. Cut the lemon halves in half again, then remove all the flesh and white pith using a small, sharp knife, leaving just the yellow skin. Slice the skin into very thin strips and set aside.

Heat the olive oil in a heavy-based saucepan over medium–low heat. Add the onion and cook, stirring, for 8 minutes, or until softened but not coloured. Add the ginger, garlic and spices and cook for a further 30 seconds. Pour in the vinegar, lemon juice and 125 ml (4 fl oz/½ cup) water, then stir in the salt. Bring to the boil, reduce the heat to a gentle simmer and cook, stirring occasionally, for 1 hour, or until the lemon skins are very tender. Increase the heat to medium–high and stir in the sugar. Cook for a further 10 minutes.

Meanwhile, prepare the stew. Heat the olive oil in a heavy-based saucepan over medium–low heat. Add the onion and cook, stirring, for 8 minutes, or until softened. Add the garlic, spices and tomato paste and stir for 1 minute.

Pour in the stock and add the potato. Bring to the boil, reduce the heat to a gentle simmer, then cover and cook for 20 minutes, or until the potato is just tender. Add the cabbage, dates, cauliflower and beans. Cover and cook for a further 10–15 minutes.

Divide the stew among serving bowls. Serve with the lemon pickle and couscous on the side, and the coriander and pistachios to sprinkle over, if desired.

To make more of a preserved lemon style relish, allow the lemon pickle to sit for at least 7 days before using.

Beetroot, red wine and borlotti bean risotto

※

When handling fresh beetroot is is a good idea to wear disposable rubber gloves to prevent the beetroot from staining your hands.

5 small beetroot (beets), about 650 g
   (1 lb 7 oz), with stems and leaves
2 tablespoons olive oil
25 g (1 oz) butter
1 large brown onion
2 garlic cloves, finely chopped
2 rosemary sprigs
1.25 litres (44 fl oz/5 cups) vegetable stock
330 g (11½ oz/1½ cups) arborio rice
250 ml (9 fl oz/1 cup) red wine
50 g (1¾ oz/⅓ cup) currants
400 g (14 oz/2 cups) tinned borlotti
   (cranberry) beans, rinsed and drained
100 g (3½ oz/1 cup) finely grated
   parmesan cheese

Trim the stems from the beetroot, leaving about 1 cm (½ inch) attached and reserving the stems and leaves. Place the beetroot in a small saucepan, cover with water, then bring to a simmer over medium heat. Cook for 50–60 minutes, or until nearly tender when pierced with a skewer, then drain well and allow to cool slightly. Using your hands, peel off the skins, then chop the beetroot and set aside.

Heat the olive oil and butter in a large saucepan over medium heat. Add the onion and garlic and cook, stirring, for 5 minutes, or until the onion is starting to soften. Add the beetroot and rosemary. Cover and cook, stirring often, for 15 minutes, or until the beetroot is tender. Chop the reserved beetroot stems and leaves and add them to the pan.

Meanwhile, bring the stock to a simmer in a saucepan, then cover, reduce heat and keep at a simmer.

Add the rice to the beetroot mixture and cook, stirring, for 2–3 minutes, or until the rice is heated through. Add the wine and stir until it has been absorbed. Add 250 ml (9 fl oz/1 cup) of the hot stock, then cook, stirring, until the stock has been absorbed. Add another 250 ml (9 fl oz/1 cup) of stock and stir until the stock has been absorbed. Continue adding the stock and stirring the rice until the stock has been almost all absorbed and the rice is just tender — the mixture should be creamy.

Stir in the currants and borlotti beans and cook for 2 minutes, or until heated through.

Divide the risotto among serving bowls, scatter with the parmesan and serve.

Preparation time: 30 minutes

Cooking time:
1 hour 40 minutes

Serves: 4–6

Preparation time: 35 minutes

Cooking time: 1 hour 55 minutes

Serves: 4

Baked ricotta-stuffed eggplant rolls

80 ml (2½ fl oz/⅓ cup) olive oil

1 brown onion, finely chopped

1 red capsicum (pepper), finely chopped

2 garlic cloves, crushed

2 tablespoons tomato paste
(concentrated purée)

125 ml (4 fl oz/½ cup) dry white wine

2 x 400 g (14 oz) tins chopped tomatoes

1 teaspoon white sugar

2 eggplants (aubergines), about 600 g
(1 lb 5 oz), cut lengthways into
5 mm (¼ inch)-thick slices

2 tablespoons lemon juice

75 g (2½ oz/¾ cup) grated
pecorino cheese

oregano, to garnish

Ricotta stuffing

400 g (14 oz/1⅔ cups) fresh
ricotta cheese

2½ tablespoons oregano, chopped

1 teaspoon finely grated lemon rind

¾ teaspoon freshly grated nutmeg

75 g (2¼ oz/¾ cup) grated
pecorino cheese

1 egg, lightly beaten

40 g (1½ oz/¼ cup) pine nuts, toasted

2 tablespoons finely chopped rinsed and
drained capers

Heat 1½ tablespoons of the olive oil in a heavy-based saucepan over medium–low heat. Add the onion and cook, stirring, for 8 minutes, or until softened. Add the capsicum and garlic and cook for 5 minutes.

Stir in the tomato paste and cook for 30 seconds, then add the wine, tomato and sugar. Increase the heat to medium and bring to the boil, then reduce the heat to low and simmer gently, stirring occasionally, for 1 hour, or until the sauce has reduced and thickened. Season to taste with sea salt and freshly ground black pepper. Keep warm.

Preheat the oven to 180°C (350°F/Gas 4). Heat a chargrill pan or barbecue hotplate to medium. Brush the eggplant slices with the remaining oil and season to taste. Chargrill in batches for 2 minutes on each side, or until golden and tender. Remove each batch to a plate and sprinkle with the lemon juice.

To make the ricotta stuffing, combine all the ingredients in a bowl and season to taste.

Lay the eggplant slices on a clean work surface. Divide the ricotta mixture among the wide ends of the eggplant slices, then roll each one into a firm roll. Place seam side down in a baking dish measuring about 28 x 19 x 6 cm (11¼ x 7½ x 2½ inches).

Spoon the tomato sauce over the eggplant rolls and sprinkle with the pecorino. Bake for 35 minutes, or until the cheese is golden and bubbling. Garnish with oregano and serve.

Broad bean, sweet potato and pea rotolo

750 g (1 lb 10 oz) orange sweet potato,
   peeled and chopped
1 tablespoon olive oil
½ teaspoon chilli flakes
235 g (8½ oz/1½ cups) frozen peas
115 g (4 oz/¾ cup) frozen broad
   (fava) beans
375 g (13 oz/1½ cups) fresh
   ricotta cheese
35 g (1¼ oz/⅓ cup) grated
   parmesan cheese
1½ teaspoons finely grated lemon rind
4 fresh lasagne sheets (each about
   10 x 14 cm/4 x 5½ inches)
40 g (1½ oz) butter
2 teaspoons lemon juice
1 tablespoon small basil leaves

Baby spinach and walnut salad
90 g (3¼ oz/2 cups) baby spinach leaves
40 g (1½ oz/⅓ cup) chopped
   toasted hazelnuts
2 tablespoons extra virgin olive oil
1½ tablespoons lemon juice

Preheat the oven to 180°C (350°F/Gas 4).

Place the sweet potato in a baking dish.
Drizzle with the olive oil, sprinkle with the chilli
flakes and season to taste with sea salt and
freshly ground black pepper. Toss to combine,
then bake for 25 minutes, or until tender.
Remove from the oven and leave to cool.

Meanwhile, cook the peas and broad beans in
a small saucepan of boiling water for 3 minutes,
or until tender. Drain. When the broad beans
are cool enough to handle, peel and discard the
skins. Leave to cool.

Combine the sweet potato, peas and broad
beans in a bowl, then roughly crush using a fork.
Add the ricotta, parmesan and lemon rind and
mix well to combine.

Place a lasagne sheet on a cutting board.
Spoon about ¼ cup of the pea mixture evenly
over the pasta, then roll up like a Swiss roll.
Brush the edges with water, and press together to
seal. Repeat with the remaining pasta and filling.
Wrap each roll tightly in plastic wrap, then foil.

Gently lower the rolls into a large saucepan
of simmering water. Place a plate on top to keep
them submerged. Cook for 25 minutes, then
remove the rolls from the water with a slotted
spoon and leave to stand for 5 minutes.

While the rolls are standing, make the baby
spinach and walnut salad. Combine the spinach
and hazelnuts in a bowl, drizzle with the olive
oil and toss gently to combine. Sprinkle with the
lemon juice and season to taste.

Just before serving, melt the butter in a frying
pan over high heat for 2 minutes, or until lightly
browned. Add the lemon juice and basil and stir
to combine. Season to taste.

Slice each rotolo into three pieces and place
on serving plates. Drizzle with the burnt butter
sauce and serve with the salad.

Preparation time: 30 minutes   **Cooking time:** 55 minutes   **Serves:** 4

Preparation time: 50 minutes
plus overnight soaking

Cooking time:
1 hour 10 minutes

Serves: 6

Chillies rellenos

12 banana chillies
250 g (9 oz/1⅔ cups) grated mozzarella
cheese
6 eggs, separated
125 g (4½ oz) plain flour
100 ml (3½ fl oz) olive oil

Red sauce
1 tablespoon olive oil
1 brown onion, thinly sliced
1 red capsicum (pepper), trimmed,
seeded and finely chopped
2 garlic cloves, crushed
1 teaspoon ground coriander
½ teaspoon ground cumin
½ teaspoon ground chilli powder
2 x 400 g (14 oz) tins chopped
tomatoes, undrained

Salsa
150g (5½ oz/¾ cup) dried black turtle
beans, soaked overnight, then drained
1 teaspoon sea salt
2 vine-ripened tomatoes, finely chopped
1 large avocado, finely chopped
2 spring onions (scallions), diagonally
thinly sliced
1–2 tablespoons lime juice
40 g (1½ oz/¼ cup) pumpkin seeds
(pepitas), toasted
1 handful coriander (cilantro) leaves,
chopped (optional)

To make the red sauce, heat the oil in a heavy-based saucepan over medium heat. Add the onion and cook, stirring, for 8 minutes, or until softened. Add the capsicum and garlic and cook, stirring often, for a further 5 minutes or until the capsicum softens. Stir in the coriander, cumin and chilli powder and cook for 30 seconds. Add the tomato, bring to the boil, reduce the heat to medium–low and simmer gently for 1 hour or until reduced and thickened to a good sauce consistency.

Meanwhile, make the salsa. Bring a saucepan of water to the boil over high heat. Add the beans and salt and cook for 40 minutes, or until tender. Drain and rinse under cold water. Set aside.

In a large bowl combine the beans, tomato, avocado, spring onion, lime juice and pumpkin seeds. Season to taste. Cover and refrigerate until needed.

Preheat the grill (broiler) to high. Place the chillies on a baking tray and grill (broil) for 4–5 minutes on each side or until the skins just blister. Transfer to a bowl, cover and cool. Very carefully remove the skins from each chilli; they will be soft and fragile. Cut the sides open to allow for the filling. Carefully remove the seeds and membrane with a small spoon.

Fill each chilli with the mozzarella. Beat the egg whites until firm peaks form. Beat the egg yolks with 2 tablespoons of the flour and season with salt. Gently fold in the egg whites to form a thick paste.

Heat the oil in a frying pan until hot. Coat the chillies in the remaining flour and dip into the batter, allowing any excess to drip off. Fry the chillies for 1–2 minutes on each side or until golden. Drain on paper towels. Divide among plates, spoon over the red sauce and serve with the salsa and chopped coriander, if desired.

INDEX

A

asparagus
asparagus and snow pea tempura   37
baked wholemeal crepes with
    asparagus and leek and basil
    cream   112
bean, asparagus and potato salad
    with smoked paprika romesco   104
aubergine *see* eggplant
avocado salsa   108

B

banh xeo   65
barley, celery and yoghurt soup   78
beans
bean, asparagus and potato salad
    with smoked paprika romesco   104
beetroot, red wine and borlotti
    bean risotto   180
broad bean and haloumi fritters
    with walnut tarator   54
broad bean, sweet potato and
    pea rotolo   184
cauliflower and white bean korma   140
Georgian bean pie   175
linguine with green beans, potato
    and mint and almond pesto   136
Mexican bean casserole on
    cornbread with avocado salsa   108
salsa   187
white bean and silverbeet timbales
    with roast tomato sauce   116
beetroot
beetroot, red wine and borlotti
    bean risotto   180
braised beetroot salad with
    goat's cheese croûtes   53
biscotti, black pepper, fennel
    and marsala   22
blue cheese
blue cheese and hazelnut butter
    pumpernickel stacks   21
blue cheese mille-feuille with glazed
    red onion and fig and cress salad   100

radicchio salad with fennel, grapefruit,
    blue cheese and almonds   81
borlotti beans   104
broccoli
kung pao with broccoli and
    peanuts   128
pad see hew   148
burghul   61

C

capsicum
capsicum sformato with radicchio
    and olive salad   25
chilled Moroccan carrot and
    capsicum soup   29
polenta and provolone soufflés with
    red wine–rosemary capsicum   139
smoked paprika romesco   104
caramelised onion tarte tatin   151
carrot
carrot and almond gougère   156
carrot pierogi with dill sour cream   13
chilled Moroccan carrot and
    capsicum soup   29
cauliflower, pickled   34
cauliflower and white bean korma   140
char siu sauce   159
cheddar soda bread with pickled
    cauliflower   34
cheese
baked ricotta-stuffed eggplant rolls   183
braised beetroot salad with goat's
    cheese croûtes   53
cheddar soda bread with pickled
    cauliflower   34
chillies rellenos   187
fried eggplant, mozzarella and
    basil sandwiches   17
green vegetable bake with pine
    nut and pecorino crumble   124
mushroom, dill and cream
    cheese coulibiac   171
olive, goat's cheese and potato
    triangles   18

polenta and provolone soufflés with
    red wine–rosemary capsicum   139
roasted pumpkin gnocchi with
    three-cheese sauce   143
watercress, walnut and goat's
    cheese salad   151
see also blue cheese; haloumi
chickpeas
chickpea, corn and semi-dried
    tomato patties with rocket salad   103
spicy chickpea pot pie   172
chilli
chillies rellenos   187
lime chilli dressing   65
tofu burgers with sweet chilli
    mayonnaise   144
Chinese hot and sour soup   85
Chinese pearl balls, steamed   9
clay pot mushrooms, tofu and
    vermicelli   120
corn
chickpea, corn and semi-dried
    tomato patties with rocket salad   103
lemongrass, corn and coconut soup   69
cornbread   108
coulibiac   171
couscous salad   152
couscous stuffing   93
crepes *see* pancakes
cumin-spiced tomato sauce   99
curry
cauliflower and white bean korma   140
dry potato curry with eggs
    and peas   132
eggplant curry   111
green vegetable curry   119

D

dipping sauces
    sesame ginger   9
    soy ginger   37
dressings and sauces
    basil oil   50
    creamy pesto   46

cumin-spiced tomato sauce 99
dill sour cream 13
egg and lemon 90
garlic mustard 81
herb mayonnaise 10
lime chilli 65
North African-spiced tomato sauce 167
orange and sherry vinegar 49
raisin dressing 53
red miso 168
red sauce 187
roast tomato sauce 116
roasted garlic aïoli 30
smoked paprika romesco 104
sweet chilli mayonnaise 144
tahini garlic sauce 73
tarragon mayonnaise 94
three-cheese sauce 143
tomato sauce 147
wasabi miso dressing 62
dry potato curry with eggs
and peas 132

E
eggplant
baked ricotta-stuffed eggplant rolls 183
eggplant curry 111
five-spice braised eggplant with
tofu and bok choy 159
fried eggplant, mozzarella and
basil sandwiches 17
tofu steak with fried eggplant,
daikon and red miso dressing 168
eggs
chillies rellenos 187
dry potato curry with eggs and peas 132
egg and lemon sauce 90
Thai eggs with sweet and
spicy sauce 74

F
fettuccine with roast fennel, saffron,
olives and breadcrumbs 131
fig and cress salad 100

five-spice braised eggplant with tofu
and bok choy 159
fried rice 176
fritto misto with tarragon
mayonnaise 94

G
galloping horses, vegetarian 33
garam masala 132
garlic
garlic mustard dressing 81
roasted garlic aïoli 30
tahini garlic sauce 73
Georgian bean pie 175
Greek red lentil and potato rissoles 123
green vegetable bake with pine
nut and pecorino crumble 124
green vegetable curry 119

H
haloumi **147**
baked turlu turlu with haloumi 147
broad bean and haloumi fritters
with walnut tarator 54
haloumi croûtes with onion, raisin
and oregano marmalade 26
harissa 29
hazelnut dukkah 89
herb mayonnaise 10
hoisin sauce 77

I, J, K
Indonesian spring rolls 82
jerusalem artichokes 89
jicama 77
kaffir lime leaves 119
kecap manis 74
kombu 41
kung pao with broccoli and peanuts 128

L
Lebanese zucchini 99
leek and basil cream 112
leeks, cooking 112

lemon pickle 179
lemongrass, corn and coconut soup 69
lemons, preserved 152
lentils
Greek red lentil and potato rissoles 123
puy lentils with chestnuts and
spinach on soft polenta 135
red lentil koftas with tahini garlic
sauce 73
Syrian lentil pizzas 14
lime chilli dressing 65
linguine with green beans, potato
and mint and almond pesto 136

M
ma hor 33
makrut leaves 119
mee rebus 163
Mexican bean casserole on
cornbread with avocado salsa 108
Middle Eastern burghul salad 61
mint and almond pesto 136
mint and ginger raita 132
mint salsa verde 86
miso broth with tofu and mushrooms 57
mushrooms
clay pot mushrooms, tofu and
vermicelli 120
miso broth with tofu and
mushrooms 57
mushroom, dill and cream
cheese coulibiac 171
mushroom caviar with olive bread 38
mushroom salad with ciabatta
croutons and mint salsa verde 86
mushroom and spinach lasagne 127

N
noodles
mee rebus 163
pad see hew 148
soba noodle salad with tofu,
radish and sesame 62
nori sheets 41

O

olive, goat's cheese and potato triangles 18

onion

caramelised onion tarte tatin 151

onion, raisin and oregano
marmalade 26

orange and sherry vinegar dressing 49

P

pad see hew 148

pancakes

baked wholemeal crepes with asparagus
and leek and basil cream 112

banh xeo 65

mini pumpkin pancakes with slow-
roasted tomatoes and creamy pesto 46

parsnip

roast parsnip, pumpkin, chestnut
and pear salad 49

vegetable skewers with parsnip
skordalia 155

pasta

broad bean, sweet potato and
pea rotolo 184

fettuccine with roast fennel, saffron,
olives and breadcrumbs 131

linguine with green beans, potato
and mint and almond pesto 136

mushroom and spinach lasagne 120

pastries

carrot and almond gougère 156

chilled tomato mousse with
sesame pastries 42

Georgian bean pie 175

mushroom, dill and cream cheese
coulibiac 171

olive, goat's cheese and potato triangles 18

silverbeet, rice and parmesan tart 160

split pea samosas 45

Persian vegetable and fruit stew 115

pierogi 13

pizza

pizza with pear, radicchio and walnuts 107

Syrian lentil pizzas 14

polenta

cornbread 108

polenta and provolone soufflés with
red wine–rosemary capsicum 139

pumpkin and polenta chips 10

puy lentils with chestnuts and
spinach on soft polenta 135

potato

bean, asparagus and potato salad
with smoked paprika romesco 104

dry potato curry with eggs and peas 132

Greek red lentil and potato rissoles 123

potato mash 172

warm jerusalem artichoke and potato
purée with hazelnut dukkah 89

pumpkin

mini pumpkin pancakes with
slow-roasted tomatoes and
creamy pesto 46

pumpkin and polenta chips 10

roast parsnip, pumpkin, chestnut
and pear salad 49

roasted pumpkin gnocchi with
three-cheese sauce 143

puy lentils with chestnuts and
spinach on soft polenta 135

Q, R

quinoa and vegetable soup 58

radicchio and olive salad 25

radicchio salad with fennel, grapefruit,
blue cheese and almonds 81

raitas 66, 132

red Asian shallots 111, 163

red lentil koftas with tahini garlic sauce 73

red miso dressing 168

rice

beetroot, red wine and borlotti
bean risotto 180

saffron rice 115

silverbeet, rice and parmesan tart 160

steamed Chinese pearl balls 9

Thai pineapple and tofu fried rice 176

rice paper rolls, Vietnamese 77

rocket salad 103

romesco, smoked paprika 104

S

saffron rice 115

salads

baby spinach and walnut 184

braised beetroot salad with goat's
cheese croûtes 53

couscous salad 152

fig and cress salad 100

Middle Eastern burghul salad 61

mushroom salad with ciabatta
croutons and mint salsa verde 86

radicchio and olive 25

radicchio salad with fennel, grapefruit,
blue cheese and almonds 81

roast parsnip, pumpkin, chestnut
and pear salad 49

rocket salad 103

soba noodle salad with tofu,
radish and sesame 62

Thai tofu salad 70

tomato and mint 18

tomato salad with mint pepper
dressing, raita and poppadoms 66

watercress, walnut and goat's
cheese 151

salt and pepper tofu with snow peas 164

sambal oelek 148

samosas, split pea 45

sauces see dressings

sesame ginger dipping sauce 9

sesame pastries 42

silverbeet

silverbeet, rice and parmesan tart 160

white bean and silverbeet timbales
with roast tomato sauce 116

skordalia 155

soba noodle salad with tofu, radish
and sesame 62

soufflés, polenta and provolone, with
red wine–rosemary capsicum 139

soup

barley, celery and yoghurt 78
chilled Moroccan carrot and
  capsicum 29
Chinese hot and sour 85
lemongrass, corn and coconut 69
miso broth with tofu and
  mushrooms 57
quinoa and vegetable 58
roast tomato, sweet potato and
  orange soup with basil oil 50
soy ginger dipping sauce 37
soy sauces 37
spiced sweet potato coils with
  couscous salad 152
spicy chickpea pot pie 172

spinach

baby spinach and walnut salad 184
mushroom and spinach lasagne 120
puy lentils with chestnuts and
  spinach on soft polenta 135
split pea samosas 45
spring rolls, Indonesian 82
sticky rice 9
stuffed vine leaves with egg
  and lemon sauce 90
sushi 41

sweet potato

broad bean, sweet potato and
  pea rotolo 184
mee rebus 163
roast tomato, sweet potato and
  orange soup with basil oil 50
spiced sweet potato coils with
  couscous salad 152
sweet potato chips 144
Syrian lentil pizzas 14

T

tahini garlic sauce 73
taleggio 135
tarragon mayonnaise 94
tempeh 148
tempura, asparagus and snow pea 37

Thai eggs with sweet and spicy sauce 74
Thai pineapple and tofu fried rice 176
Thai tofu salad 70
timbales 116

tofu

clay pot mushrooms, tofu and
  vermicelli 120
five-spice braised eggplant with
  tofu and bok choy 159
miso broth with tofu and
  mushrooms 57
salt and pepper tofu with
  snow peas 164
soba noodle salad with tofu, radish
  and sesame 62
Thai pineapple and tofu fried rice 176
Thai tofu salad 70
tofu burgers with sweet chilli
  mayonnaise 144
tofu steak with fried eggplant,
  daikon and red miso dressing 168
Vietnamese rice paper rolls 77

tomato

chilled tomato mousse with sesame
  pastries 42
cumin-spiced tomato sauce 99
mini pumpkin pancakes with
  slow-roasted tomatoes and
  creamy pesto 46
North African-spiced tomato
  sauce 167
roast tomato, sweet potato and
  orange soup with basil oil 50
roast tomato sauce 116
stuffed tomatoes with baked
  yoghurt 93
Thai eggs with sweet and spicy
  sauce 74
tomato salad with mint pepper
  dressing, raita and poppadoms 66
tomato sauce 147
Tunisian vegetable stew with lemon
  pickle 179
turlu turlu, baked, with haloumi 147

V

vegetables

baked turlu turlu with haloumi 147
Persian vegetable and fruit stew 115
chargrilled vegetable platter with
  roasted garlic aïoli 30
green vegetable bake with pine
  nut and pecorino crumble 124
green vegetable curry 119
quinoa and vegetable soup 58
Tunisian vegetable stew with
  lemon pickle 179
vegetable skewers with parsnip
  skordalia 155
vegetarian galloping horses 33
vegetarian 'meatballs' in North
  African-spiced tomato sauce 167
vegetarian oyster sauce 120
Vietnamese rice paper rolls 77

W

walnut shortcrust pastry 175
walnut tarator 54
warm jerusalem artichoke and potato
  purée with hazelnut dukkah 89
wasabi miso dressing 62
watercress, walnut and goat's
  cheese salad 151
white bean and silverbeet timbales
  with roast tomato sauce 116
white miso paste 57
wholemeal crepes, baked, with
  asparagus and leek and
  basil cream 112

Y, Z

yellow bean sauce 163

yoghurt

barley, celery and yoghurt soup 78
minted yoghurt 99
stuffed tomatoes with baked
  yoghurt 93
zucchini, stuffed, with minted yoghurt
  and cumin-spiced tomato sauce 99

Published in 2011 by Murdoch Books Pty Limited

Murdoch Books Australia
Pier 8/9
23 Hickson Road
Millers Point NSW 2000
Phone: +61 (0) 2 8220 2000
Fax: +61 (0) 2 8220 2558
www.murdochbooks.com.au

Murdoch Books UK Limited
Erico House, 6th Floor
93–99 Upper Richmond Road
Putney, London SW15 2TG
Phone: +44 (0) 20 8785 5995
Fax: +44 (0) 20 8785 5985
www.murdochbooks.co.uk

Publishing director: Chris Rennie
Publisher: Kylie Walker
Project editor: Anneka Manning
Food editor: Leanne Kitchen
Copy editor: Katri Hilden
Cover concept: Yolande Gray
Design concept: Emilia Toia
Designer: Katy Wall
Photographer: Natasha Milne
Stylist: Sarah O'Brien
Food preparation: Kristin Buesing
Recipes developed by Nick Banbury, Peta Dent, Fiona Hammond, Leanne Kitchen,
Kirrily La Rosa, Kim Meredith, Angela Tregonning and the Murdoch Books test kitchen.

Text, design and photography copyright © Murdoch Books Pty Limited 2010

All rights reserved. No part of this publication may be reproduced, stored in a retrieval system or transmitted in any form or by any means, electronic, mechanical, photocopying, recording or otherwise, without the prior written permission of the publisher.

National Library of Australia Cataloguing-in-Publication
National Library of Australia Cataloguing-in-Publication entry
Title: My kitchen : Vegetarian : it's not all beans and tofu.
ISBN: 9781741964486 (hbk.)
Series: My kitchen series.
Notes: Includes index.
Subjects: Vegetarian cooking.
Dewey Number: 641.5636

PRINTED IN CHINA.

IMPORTANT: Those who might be at risk from the effects of salmonella poisoning (the elderly, pregnant women, young children and those suffering from immune deficiency diseases) should consult their doctor with any concerns about eating raw eggs.

OVEN GUIDE: You may find cooking times vary depending on the oven you are using. For fan-forced ovens, as a general rule, set the oven temperature to 20°C (35°F) lower than indicated in the recipe.